THE PERGAMON ENGLISH LIBRARY

EDITORIAL DIRECTORS: GEORGE ALLEN & BORIS FORD

EXECUTIVE EDITOR: ESMOR JONES

PUBLISHER: ROBERT MAXWELL, M.C., M.P.

MAGAZINES TEENAGERS READ

MAGAZINES TEENAGERS READ

WITH SPECIAL REFERENCE TO
Trend, Jackie and Valentine

by

CONNIE ALDERSON

THE QUEEN'S AWARD
TO INDUSTRY 1966

PERGAMON PRESS

PERGAMON PRESS LTD.

OXFORD · LONDON · EDINBURGH
NEW YORK · TORONTO · SYDNEY

First Edition 1968   Copyright © 1968   CONNIE ALDERSON
Library of Congress Catalog Card No 67–30562
Printed in Great Britain by Dawson & Goodall Ltd., Bath

08 003473 X

Contents

v

vi   CONTENTS

List of Illustrations

Foreword

Magazines Teenagers Read started out as the Special Study require-
ment for an in-service course in Further Education taken at Garnett
College. Mrs. Dryland who lectures in Sociology and Education at
Garnett College gave Mrs. Alderson much encouragement and
support. In a sense the book did not begin there; it is rather the
result of twelve years' teaching of so-called non-academic pupils
in secondary modern schools and Day Release Classes in Colleges
of Further Education. Her book is an angry book, with few
holds barred, written by an extremely able and sensitive teacher.
It does not claim to be sociological, neither does it meet the demands
of the social survey. Yet I suggest that it will spark off more syste-
matic study by those who have public funds and two or three years
to think and do. Mrs. Alderson's book was written under quite
other circumstances.

Whilst it is true that we do not know, in the round, the effects
of the literary, auditory and visual styles of the mass media upon
young people during their pre-occupation with the teenage scene
and even less of the effects upon their future development, it is
appalling that our schools continue to create the possibilities for
such a market. Let us be quite clear, this is not the fault of individual
teachers. Whilst public enquiries are able to report that 49% of
all secondary modern schools are materially grossly inadequate;
that 79% of all such schools in slum and problem areas are in a
similar plight; that such schools are unable to both obtain and
retain staff; that the educational context often robs both teachers
and taught of self-respect and social significance; then this situation
will continue. The mid-nineteenth century created a lumpen proletariat out of the factory system, the mid-twentieth century may well
create an educational proletariat out of the twilight of the submerged
streams of our secondary schools.

The myths, rituals and codes of teenagers may well have their
source in structural changes in the nature of our society but the

contents of this culture and the response to it do not carry the same inevitability. Perhaps Mrs. Alderson's book might do more to open up the issue of the *educationally* deprived than formal statistical reports. Let us stop making the problem safe through the categories of the sixties, the Newsom Child, the culturally deprived, the linguistically deprived, Compensatory Education. To take the last term, we cannot talk about compensatory education where children in the first place do not receive an education. It is too easy to complain about individual teachers and the shortcomings of their training; the problem goes much deeper than this. Are we prepared to increase the total proportion of the National Income spent on education and to increase the proportion we spend on children where there may be no visible, measurable, economic return? Are we prepared to think through a coherent curriculum, an appropriate pedagogy and to create the schools which make this possible in order to prevent educational deprivation? We do no less for the educationally privileged.

Maybe Mrs. Alderson's book will help.

London, 1967   BASIL B. BERNSTEIN

Acknowledgements

MY GRATEFUL acknowledgements are due to Bob, Jenny, Judy and Jim. I should like to thank Professor Basil Bernstein for reading the original manuscript, and also Mr. David Perrin and Mr. Harry Waite. The questionnaires could not have been completed without the active co-operation of the Heads and staff of Mellow Lane School, Woodfield County School, Twickenham County School and Gunnersbury Boys' Grammar School. I should like to thank the local education authorities and governors of these schools. I am also grateful to my colleagues at Isleworth Polytechnic.

The author would also like to thank City Magazines Ltd. for permission to reprint material from *Trend* and Fleetway Publications Ltd. and D. C. Thomson & Co. Ltd. for permission to reprint material from *Valentine* and from *Jackie*, and for their co-operation in providing the original material.

The photograph of The Cream is reproduced by permission of Pictorial Press Ltd.

The anti-smoking advertisement is Crown copyright, reproduced with the permission of the Controller of H.M. Stationery Office.

CHAPTER 1

Popular magazines available today
The three teenage magazines studied
intensively

. . . abbanysh and exclude such as ratheyr
may be called blotterature thenne literature.
(Colet of St. Paul's School)

"I'm glad the holiday's over even though we're going back to
work."

"Yes, now we can get back to the old routine."

"It's funny, Janice, I've been thinking, you go to the pictures
with Derek on a Saturday and I go with Colin on a Sunday, and it's
his house on a Sunday for you two, and my house on a Saturday for
us two."

"Yes, and we all meet at the Club on a Tuesday."

"It's nice to be back doing what we always do . . ."

The familiar is comforting and routine makes for a stable life, but
it is rather saddening that two girls of 16 or 17 feel unsafe when
it is broken for a bank holiday. The conversation was taking place
between the two girls at a bus stop. Both were clutching fresh copies
of *Jackie* and *Valentine* and they could have been taken from the
strip stories of these teenage magazines. They were the sixties'
product of what Northcliffe referred to when he said to Max
Pemberton in 1883:

The Board Schools are turning out hundreds of thousands of boys
and girls annually who are anxious to read. They do not care for the
ordinary newspaper. They have no interest in society, but they will
read anything which is simple and sufficiently interesting. The man
who has produced this *Tit-bits* has got hold of a bigger thing than he

I

imagines. He is only at the beginning of a development which is going to change the whole face of journalism. I shall try to get in with him.

Today the big business men behind the teenage magazines have responded to the restricted lives of millions of young people. While educationists write in halycon terms of the new methods of teaching English, of creativity and spontaneity—in fact an entirely new approach to the use of language, and teachers of liberal studies in further education battle to give something of the cultural side of life to young workers, the men who give the teenagers what they appear to really want to read are those who produce the magazines.

Faced with a class of day-release students in further education the teacher looks at his time-table and sees "English Literature". This is what teacher-training text books call "a challenge". Some of the students will be ex-grammar who might like to have another try at GCE O-level literature which they did not obtain at school, the majority will be ex-secondary modern pupils who will tolerate the "literature" doled out to them in the class-room but whose real allegiance will be to the magazines of the cheapest and most trivial kind. It was this allegiance which prompted the investigation into the three most popular teenage magazines and the writing of this book. Most girls appear to go through a phase of reading teenage magazines, but it is the young worker and less academically minded school-girl at whom the magazines are aimed. In fact, the readership is aimed at the less educated, the less articulate and the underprivileged. The girl whose mother reads the magazines is likely to continue reading them herself until she graduates to a woman's magazine. In discussing the teenage magazines, the girls who read them admit that the stories are "soppy", "not true to life"—in fact unconvincing and superficial, but they have a strong allegiance to them which it is difficult to shake. The *Children's Newspaper*, which ceased publication in 1966, carried its own death note in its very name—"children". The magazines aimed at the girl from 7 to 12 are becoming more and more precocious, and the pop world stretches down from the teenager to the young child.

The Newsom Report which deals with less able children states quite definitely that:

> All pupils, including those of very limited attainments, need the civilising experience of contact with great literature.

Teachers should not be afraid to carry this out. The girls who read the teenage magazines *do like reading*, and it is wicked to write them off as being incapable of appreciating anything better. The magazine proprietors do this but should teachers? If the girls like to read of love, give them love. It isn't difficult to find in "great literature". *Madame Bovary, Esther Waters* and the contemporary *The Millstone** are but a few examples.

A rag-week notice in a Polytechnic recently caught my eye. It read

LOVE
Is a many - splendoured thing and I
refuse to make jokes about it —

I can recall a day-release class greeting the announcement of the proposed reading of *Jane Eyre* with groans and cries of horror:

"It's dry."
"It's long and boring."
"It's old fashioned."
"It's dead dull."

I gave them a blurb: melodrama, love, mad wife, emancipation of women, drama at the marriage altar, and they agreed to try it. Eventually most of the class was completely won over, and when Jane is told by St. John Rivers that she was "formed for labour not for love" one of the most difficult students shouted out spontaneously "What a cheek!", and from there the discussion was fast and lively.

Some pupils and young students respond better to modern fiction than to the classics for which there may be a built-in hostility. But whatever the book it should never be second rate. To offer the second rate because it will be more easily welcomed is to give in and go half-way towards magazine reading. Yet, one should not under-rate the tremendous influence exerted by the cheap magazines.

It is a depressing reflection on our educational system that readers respond to the limited and totally superficial content of such "literature". Girls who were interviewed said again and again that they enjoyed the feeling of belonging, and the teenage magazines

* Margaret Drabble.

do give them this sense of being part of a special group, a special sub-culture. A century ago, one of H.M. inspectors, Matthew Arnold, predicted:

> Plenty of people will try to give the masses, as they call them, an intellectual food prepared and adapted in the way they think proper for the actual condition of the masses. The ordinary popular literature is an example of this way of working on the masses.

The 1870 Education Act taught people how to read, and the big boys jumped in with the popular press which has continued to expand, and the popular or tabloid daily and Sunday newspapers have increased their readership far more than the "quality" newspapers. The popularity of the *Daily Mirror* is evident in the figures taken from the questionnaires dealt with in Chapter 7. In the last 20 years many small, independent newspapers have been swallowed up by the big combines, and the trend has been one of standardisation not individuality.

A glance at any railway bookstall today will show the variety of magazines on sale. These could be classified as:

1. Trade magazines such as *Confectioners' News*, etc. There are about 700 such magazines and these do not include trade union journals which are circulated to members and not on sale to the general public. In this group might come magazines for professional groups such as *The Lancet* or *Architectural Review*.
2. Magazines dealing with hobbies and specialist interests such as *Amateur Gardener*, *Practical Motorist*, *Plays and Players* or *Model Boats*.
3. Religious and minority group magazines such as *The Universe* or *The Humanist*.
4. The serious weeklies—*The Listener*, *New Statesman*, etc.
5. Women's magazines of all types from the quality *Vogue* to the *Woman's Weekly* type.
6. So-called "family" magazines such as *Week-end* and *Reveille*.
7. Serious quarterly magazines such as *Encounter*, *Political Quarterly*, *Which* and *Where*.
8. The English-type magazines for younger children—*Beano*, *Dandy*, *Judy* and *Princess*.
9. English teenage magazines—*Valentine*, *Jackie* and *Romeo*.
10. American magazines—*Batman* and *Batboy*, *Monster*, etc.

11. Sex magazines aimed at men and boys—*Penthouse*, *Stag* and *Topless*.
12. Miscellaneous magazines which might include the *Radio Times*, and the mightiest of them all—*TV Times*.

Nearly 100 years after the first Education Act the producers of magazines for teenagers and near-teenagers are developing and intensifying the ideas of George Newnes and Northcliffe. Teenage magazines began with *Marilyn* in 1955 and have grown in number and circulation. There are now about ten with a combined circulation of 3 million and the number of readers is more like 9 millions. The survey carried out among school-children reveals that a magazine is read by a number of children and not just by the child who buys it. The teenage magazines are nothing like the *Peg's Paper* type of magazine of pre-war days. For one thing the readership begins at a much lower age, and for another the dominant interest is in pop stars and the pop scene. This is something completely new and is not confined to teenage magazines. Magazines intended for younger girls are dominated by the pop scene in the same way.

The three teenage magazines which have been studied for a period of 8 months are:

Trend, published by City Magazines Limited;
Valentine published by Fleetway Publications Limited; and
Jackie, published by D. C. Thomson & Co. Ltd.

A journalist from one of these three magazines said that the readership age began at 10 plus and this was confirmed by the survey. The 3 magazines were chosen mainly because they have the biggest circulation figures. The 1964 figures for *Trend* were 378,081. *Valentine*'s circulation was given as 375,732, but this magazine is now combined with *Marilyn* which had a circulation in 1964 of 129,515. D. C. Thomson do not reveal the circulation figures for *Jackie*, but newsagents place it high on their best-selling list, and the advertisement rates indicate that this is so. When the figures for the survey were analysed it was found that *Jackie* was amongst the most popular of the teenage magazines. *Trend* is the most sophisticated of the 3, its fashion features are good and it has a lower percentage of strip stories. At the end of the 8 months' study of the 3 magazines, on 19 March 1966, *Boyfriend* changed its name to *Trend and Boyfriend*

'Much Too Much'

(*Trend* is printed in large print on the front page; *and Boyfriend* is in small print).* The movement towards a more sophisticated magazine is quite clear in *Trend*. Although the study of *Trend* in this work is now somewhat historical, the changeover emphasises the readiness with which proprietors are ready to back new developments.

The 3 magazines follow a similar make-up. They contain:

1. Photographs of pop stars.
2. Strip-story romances.
3. Short, printed stories (as opposed to strip stories).
4. Features and gossip about pop stars.
5. Letters from readers asking for information about pop stars.
6. Problem letters from readers.
7. Fashion, shopping and beauty hints.
8. Miscellaneous items such as short love poems, horoscopes, competitions linked with advertising, and *Trend* ran a printed historical romance serial.
9. Advertisements.

The ration of contents is:

	Trend	Jackie	Valentine
	per cent	per cent	per cent
Picture strip stories	20	30	40
Advertisements	15	10	3
Pictures of pop stars	10	10	10
Printed stories	10	5	5
Printed historical serial	5	–	–
Pop gossip with pictures	5	17	17
Letters dealing with pop stars	5	–	10
Problem letters	3	5	4
Humorous letters from readers	–	5	–
Fashion, beauty and shopping hints	17	12	4
Competitions, illustrations for printed stories, astrology, poems, miscellaneous	10	6	7
	100	100	100

* The name *Trend* will be used throughout this study, but for references before March 1966 read *Boyfriend*.

The pop-star content is actually higher than the figures show because their signatures and names appear on some of the problem-letter pages. They appear on the fashion pages, and in *Valentine* every strip-story has the same title as the name of a current pop song and a picture of the star or group appears at the beginning of the story.

CHAPTER 2

Analysis of stories in Valentine, Jackie and Trend

STOCK SITUATIONS OF PLOTS; TABOOS; CLASS
RIGIDITY; MORALITY; READER IDENTIFICATION;
DEFINITION OF "SUCCESS"; ANTI-INTELLECTUAL
ATTITUDE; SOCIAL MORES

> . . . in general, people look not for new experiences in the
> mass-media, but for a repetition and an elaboration of their
> old experiences into which they can more easily project them-
> selves.
>
> (PAUL LAZARSFELD, American Sociologist)

SINCE 1950 many new magazines, for children and teenagers, have
come on to the market and they have been very successful. One
reason is that they use the technique common in American magazines, of strip-stories. Reading matter is reduced to a minimum and
placed in little balloons issuing from the mouths of the characters.
Many children do not read the words at all. I have watched them
study the pictures, and they say, as confirmed by George H.
Pumphrey,* that they go back and read the words later. Adults
who are accustomed to reading printed matter find the reading of
strip-stories tiring, but children who are used to strip-stories will
read them with great concentration. In addition to magazines
there are cheap paper-backed booklets on the market which contain
nothing but strip-stories.

The plots or stock situations in *Valentine, Jackie* and *Trend* follow
regular patterns. The most common is that of wish-fulfilment—the
girl gets boy, but not only a boy but the RIGHT boy. The girl who is
not enjoying a constant round of dating with Saturday night being

---

* Children's comics.

the most important, is unsuccessful, and in the story she meets a boy and eventually finds that she loves him. The word "love" is thoroughly debased in the context of the stories, and together with the word "dreams" is used more frequently than any other word.

Another common situation is used when a girl meets a boy outside her normal social circle. In the end she has to reject him for this reason. Outside the normal social circle can mean that a boy is studying and therefore is unable to date the girl regularly, or he may have a job which takes him away from home and leaves the girl without an escort. In this case the girl is pictured as being lonely and ashamed to tell her friends at the office that she has not been taken out on Saturday night. All stories contain strong reader identification. This stricture applied to boys who have strong interests not shared by the girl. They are unsuitable for "true love" and have to be rejected. A boy is a "wolf" or a "vulture" when he has a number of girl friends and is not prepared to be faithful to one. He is rejected as unsuitable. This plot sometimes results in a non-fulfilment situation which ends with the girl crying but hoping for a future where her dreams will come true and she will meet a boy who comes up to her expectations.

An example of wish-fulfilment where the girl gets not only the right boy but the boy next door is given in *Valentine*. The story begins in the prescribed *Valentine* manner with a picture of a pop group, The Rolling Stones, singing one of their numbers, "Gotta Get Away", which is also the title of the story. Linda, the heroine, has always liked "the boy next door", Paul, and had disliked his elder brother Chris. The boys and their family emigrated to Australia and Linda wrote to Paul for a number of years. She was delighted when she heard that the family was going to return to live in the same district. When they came back, all the members of the family, except Paul, got new jobs and settled down. Paul was restless and discontented. He was envious that his family had obtained "cushy" jobs and said: "Nobody wants to know about me."

His attitude irritated Linda who found herself developing a growing affection for Chris. Paul decided to emigrate to Canada on his own. He was obviously a boy of the "Gotta Get Away" type. Linda waved him off at the station and said she would write to him, but this time she was not prepared to wait because: "I have MY dreams too."

The last picture in the strip showed Chris and Linda in each other's arms. She had discovered that:

> All Paul needed was our admiration and attention. Well, he had it, but Chris had my Heart . . . and always would.

This situation where the girl is involved with a boy, and at the very end of the story finds out that he is not the right one, is used frequently. It is quite common for the girl to be in love with one boy for two and seven-eighths pages, and fall in love with another in the last picture of the strip. The fact that Paul was restless and discontented also placed him in a precarious position. Boys who are difficult, moody or do not conform in any way to the image of the regular, steady boy, are not suitable for routine dating and true love.

"The girl in his life", a strip-story from *Jackie*, presents almost the same situation. Here, the heroine, Jenny, is pictured waiting at the station for her aunt to meet her. She had sent her aunt a telegram saying she would be arriving for new year, but she is not sure whether the telegram reached her aunt in time. Jenny had been hoping that her boy friend, Colin, would ask her to the new year's ball. Colin is a boy who has often kept her wondering whether he would take her out, and this time she was tired of waiting for the invitation so she had decided to leave London and go to her aunt's. The weather is cold and wintry, and in the waiting room at the station Jenny sees Alistair, a childhood friend. He gives her a lift in his van to her aunt's house. On the way there Jenny tells him about Colin, and Alistair says:

> Does this chap make a practice of keeping you hanging around while he decides where to hand out his favours?

Jenny learns from her aunt and uncle that Alistair is sad because he loves a girl who does not bother with him. This awakens Jenny's interest in him. At a party that evening she observes his reactions to other girls and realises that it is she herself whom he loves, but he did not look at Jenny once because she had been "cruel and heartless" to him.

The next day Jenny receives a letter from Colin saying that he had intended to take her to the ball and that he was surprised that she had left her digs so suddenly. Jenny tears up the letter saying:

What a mess I've made of things. Alistair's made it plain he's no time for me and Colin's taken me for granted once too often.

Suddenly Alistair appears and the last picture shows Alistair and Jenny kissing. He has always loved her, and she realises that she has really loved him all the time.

The stories contain positive and negative elements in common. Reader identification has been mentioned and this is a common denominator. There are certain forbidden subjects which are never mentioned. These are common to the romantic stories in the cheaper women's weekly magazines, but the boundaries in the teenage magazines are even narrower. Anne Britton and Marion Collins, who have both been fiction editors of women's magazines, advise in their guide to would-be writers, *Romantic Fiction*, that reader identification is the most important aspect of women's magazine stories. They point out that most women like a story with an escapist quality, yet the plots must not exceed the realms of possibility. In a section head "Taboos" they mention the subjects which must be avoided in case of giving offence to readers. The taboo subjects are:

> Drunkenness
> Deformity
> Illegitimacy
> Colour and religion
> Divorce

From a study of the fiction in the teenage magazines I would add the following to the list:

> Politics
> Sex as opposed to "romance"
> Current affairs
> World affairs

To be fair to the women's weekly magazines, they have expanded their range of subjects as far as articles and features are concerned.

In the fiction world of *Jackie*, *Valentine* and *Trend* there are no coloured people, no sick or infirm people, no poor people, no fat people and no children. False as they may have been, the romantic pulp magazines of pre-war days did introduce their readers to the "enchanted East", but the identification level in teenage magazines is kept within tight and narrow bounds.

'The Girl in his Life'—Jackie, 1 January 1966

'The Girl in his Life'

Valentine breaks away from the usual formula in a printed serial called "Who can I turn to?" As in the strip-stories, the title is the name of a song which in this was a favourite of one of the few girl pop singers—Dusty Springfield. Her photograph appears at the top of the serial each week. This story, although simply told on "Cinderella" lines, is, in comparison with the strip-stories, far more complex and interesting. Little orphan Annie Farrow is 17 and runs away from her guardian. An unusual note is introduced here as the guardian is Mrs. Draykeller, a woman in charge of a home for delinquent girls. She had rescued Annie from Battersea when the girl was orphaned, and had brought her to live with her in the lodge attached to the Girls' Home. Annie said of her new guardian:

> Mrs. Draykeller—Auntie, was famous. She was so good, so kind, she never had a failure. Well, hardly ever. She was sort of Matron and Principal and Mother Superior and everything at Spofforths (the Home).
> Sometimes she used to lecture at Universities and appear on the telly and all sorts, as an expert on looking after girls.

There is a hint of irony and humour here, and humour is noticeably lacking in most of the stories.

Mrs. Draykeller, whom, we realise, is incapable of a personal relationship, wants to send Annie to live with a Colonel and his family. Annie's father was batman to the Colonel and once saved his life. Annie is befriended by the fiance of the Colonel's daughter. Class structures are definite. Annie says of Mark, the fiance:

> He had that nice rather posh voice. Of course, he was ever so posh as well. Never mind, I was going to a posh home myself now. I could learn the ways. Given time it might all start to come naturally. Maybe he'd never even notice the difference one day.

There is an honesty here which is missing from most of the other stories. Annie ruminates on her new clothes and new hair-do, and feels that underneath she has not changed. She says to Mark: "This sort of gear don't belong to me. I'm a mess. Go on. Say it."

This story, which applies to the majority, is written from the woman's angle. Since Richardson, who also wrote from the woman's angle, published *Pamela*, women have always been notorious fiction readers.

The first few chapters of "Who can I turn to?" are interesting compared with the thin plots of the other stories, but as the months progressed, the story lost any sense of continuity and failed to reach a satisfying point of suspense at which to end every week.

In "Time to say goodbye", a strip-story from *Jackie*, Bill is not rejected because he is "posh". Judy, the heroine is experiencing difficulty because Bill's parents want him to study to be an accountant, and dislike his going out regularly instead of staying at home to study. It is unusual to see a picture of an older person in the strip stories. In this one there are two pictures of Bill's father, who is shown as a sour, aged man with deep lines on his face and a grim expression. The story makes it quite clear that boys whose studying interferes with dating are not satisfactory. Judy has to reject Bill because:

> ... my love for you can't stay still for two years; it's alive, it's vital for now. Two years. It sounds a life-time, doesn't it? But maybe—just maybe, we'll meet up again—maybe our dream will come true.

Success is depicted in one way only—that of getting the boy friend to agree to engagement or marriage. There is no hint in the above story that Judy could have encouraged Bill to study. He was not available for constant dating; therefore he was not eligible to be a boy friend.

Values of the real world do not exist. The background of the girls working in offices is monotonous. The reader is seldom told the type of industry, and the office exists in the story merely as a place where girls meet to talk over their love experiences or as a possible meeting place for new boy friends.

The anti-intellectual or anti-serious element is strong. In "Saturday strangers", another strip-story, Betty meets Brian at the launderette. He takes her out once, but explains that he is a student at the local college of science, and that he is sitting his final examinations in 6 weeks' time. Betty suffers every Monday morning as the girls in the office tell each other what they did the previous Saturday evening while she has to invent outings. The cult of going out on Saturday night is strong and is emphasised in this story. Betty waits for Brian despite misunderstandings about the Saturday dates. She manages to get through the 6 weeks and says: "I must have been blind not to see that true love can override everything."

Mention is made that Brian, being a student, did not have the means to take his girl to exciting places, but usually it is the time

'Time to say Goodbye'

element, not the money element, which is stressed when a boy is studying.

"Ring through my nose", a strip-story from *Trend*, deserves a mention because in this story the girl gives up her boy friend because he is domineering and takes no notice of her wishes. Another frequently recurring theme is the importance laid on the engagement ring. (Advertisements for engagement rings are prominent in every issue of the magazine.) The immaturity of the strip-story heroines is brought out in "Ring through my nose" when the girl says: "Being engaged must be the most marvellous thing—even better than the wedding day."

The boundaries of the social circle are narrow and are rarely exceeded. There is very little social mobility in the fiction and girls seldom accept boys from outside their own background for very long. "Come to me" is a strip story from *Valentine* which illustrates this class rigidity. It begins with a picture of Cilla Black who features the song (Cilla Black is one of the much smaller group of successful girl pop singers). Gwen, the heroine, describes herself thus: "This is me at the office, a sophisticated girl-about-town."

She is shown wearing a slinky black sleeveless dress and standing next to her typewriter. The next picture shows Gwen in her other role. Wearing a duffle coat she is riding her bicycle in the pouring rain, delivering newspapers at 6 a.m. She explains why she has to have two jobs.

It is because her employer's son has recently joined the firm, and has asked Gwen and her friend, Freda, to parties and week-ends in the country. Both girls have to buy new clothes, and Freda even hires a car to take her to the country house. Gwen economises by asking the faithful Harry Blake, her newsagent employer, to drive her to the country station in his van, and from there she hires a taxi to drive up to the big country house. Alighting from the taxi she explains to Ronald Wilberforce Landsdowne: "So annoying! My car broke down."

In spite of desperate efforts, Ronald Wilberforce Landsdowne does not really notice Gwen or Freda, and eventually, in the last picture, Gwen realises that she really loves the faithful Harry Blake. She gives up her job in the office to work for him full time and, presumably, be his wife. All the stories end with the promise of marriage but are never developed any further.

In a similar stock situation, the story "Loving for kicks—or for keeps" tells how Carol was dazzled by the glamorous life led by

'Ring through my Nose'—Trend, 11 December 1965

Dave Coventry, the motor-racing driver, but in the end she accepts the boy who lived near and had a cheap, old car: "Dear, proud Brian, who had nothing to offer but love."

The emphasis here is that Brian was always around, while Dave, the racing driver, was always going away and leaving Carol on her own.

A similar situation is reversed in "If I needed someone" which is also a title of a song sung by The Hollies, and carries a picture of this group on the front page of *Valentine*. In the opening pictures Hazel is shown in a hospital bed saying: "It's gone, everything I ever wanted from life."

Flashbacks show Hazel a week ago when she had just obtained " that fab. secretarial job in Spain". Hazel falls down the stairs at the tube station and breaks her leg. She has to stay in hospital for 3 weeks and meanwhile the "fab. job" cannot be kept open for her.

At the hospital she meets Joe who is sympathetic to her. Later he tells her that his knee is injured as a result of a car crash and it might never be right again. Hazel feels she is much luckier than he and becomes friendly with Joe; in fact, she is not looking forward to leaving hospital: "We've had such fun, Joe. I dread going back to my old routine life."

Just before she leaves hospital, Joe tells Hazel that there is a big improvement in his health and the doctors say he might be able to leave soon. They embrace and Hazel goes home where her mother tells her that there has been a telephone call for her about the job in Spain; the girl who took her place is ill. At first Hazel is delighted and she conjures up a vision of herself sitting on a Spanish beach with a handsome young man. She says to herself: "This is what you wanted, isn't it? Warm beaches, sunlight, moving in a glamorous set . . ."

Somehow she does not feel so happy about it as she thought she would, and then she realises it is because she would have to leave Joe. In the last picture she is in his arms saying: "Don't ever let me go again, darling."

Joe says: "That would be like throwing away my luck for ever."

Rejection of "wolves" or "vultures" who are too fresh with girls is a recognised situation. *Valentine* published a strip-story called "That means a lot" (song popularised by P. J. Proby). Sylvia is looking for the perfect boy friend. She cuts pieces from photographs of old boy friends and contrives to form the face of her ideal boy. At a party an amazing thing happens—she meets a boy who looks like her dream boy. She asks her current, rather dull boy friend to introduce her and she soon finds herself alone with him. He wastes no time in trying to kiss her, which shocks Sylvia, and she returns to her quiet boy friend whom she describes as:

> My perfect man at last. He's not like ANY of the other boys I
> knew . . . Just a boy with a heart of gold . . . and you can't photo-
> graph that.

The effect of the thin, superficial structure of the stories with a choice of two endings, either catching the right boy or of being resigned to tears until the right boy comes along, is one of frustration and leads to the desire to read another story in the hope that it might prove more interesting. Very occasionally there is a strip-story with a different background, but the conventions adhered to are still iron cast.

"It's my life", a song put over by The Animals, is the title of a strip-story in *Valentine*. It is an example of a couple who *both* step outside their social circle, reject it and are happy with each other.

Gay Turner is portrayed as a girl who is always bored at parties because she is shy and unable to join in. She realises that she is not being invited to parties any more, and is attracted to an advertisement in a local newspaper which says:

> Are YOU the outcast at the party? Are you a social misfit? Let
> Confidence Unlimited put you right.

She follows up the advertisement and finds herself in a small office with Jack, a handsome young man who runs Confidence Unlimited. She tells him her story and he says: "Just shut your eyes and keep saying: I'm beautiful! I'm witty! I'm as good as anyone! "

"It seemed to work," said Gay, and acquired confidence in the next picture. Acquaintance with culture and general information which were necessary for conversation were dealt with in one picture where Gay is practising: "And what do you think of the situation in Red China, My Lord?"

The couple practise dancing in Jack's office, and the next picture shows them in evening dress, arriving at a grand house. In the ball room Gay tries out her Red China piece and gets this reply from a distinguished old man: "Hrrmph! Well can't say I've thought much of it young lady, too busy with me polo you know."

'It's my Life'—Valentine, 11 December 1965

'It's my Life'

It is obvious that Gay is dazzled with her success for in the next picture she says to Jack: "It's been the most wonderful evening of my life, Jack, and all thanks to you."

Tragedy strikes in the next picture which is a large one taking the space of four normal-sized strips. The couple are asked to leave when it is discovered that Jack gate-crashed the party. Outside the grand house Gay leaves him, after asking for her money back . . . and . . . "I actually thought I'd fallen in love with him."

The next day Gay goes to Jack's office to collect the money she has paid him for the course with Confidence Unlimited. She finds that two men are taking away his office furniture. Jack confesses that Confidence Unlimited had one client—herself. He tells Gay that he has never been able to get a decent job because he has no confidence. She realises that she now has enough confidence for two and is in love with Jack. She ends the story by saying: "Who cares about all those parties anyway? Two's a party when in love."

The social mores introduced are coffee, coffee-bars, soft drinks at parties, no alcohol and very little of smoking of cigarettes. A recent competition in *The New Statesman* asked readers to give suggestions on differences between the working and middle-classes. One of the winners made the point that middle-classes drink coffee (in England, of course) and the working classes drink tea. This does not apply in teenage magazines where the coffee-bar and drinking of coffee is a sub-culture which has taken the place of the public house. Office parties feature largely in the stories, especially Christmas parties and parties at the houses of friends. It is certainly true that young people go to a great many parties nowadays, especially on Saturday nights, but in London, especially, they are usually informal parties. Teenage magazines have their biggest circulation in the provinces where young people may dress up more for parties. In London and the home counties they appear to deliberately "dress down".

Dating is an all-important feature. Boys and girls usually meet at places outside home. Boys bring girls to the door of their homes and sometimes kiss goodbye. "My girl" goes steady with "My boy", and they do not join in family activities. At the office, girls discuss their experiences with other girls and the girl who has no steady boy friend is encouraged to remedy this. She is definitely made to feel that she has failed if she has no boy friend.

Although the stories adhere to moral conventions of a rigid type and seldom, if ever, flout them, they are basically amoral. The heroines of the stories are never really involved in a moral decision. They reject boys whom they classify as "wolves" or "dead fresh", but their role is to get engaged or "go steady" with the right type of boy as soon as possible, and all decisions are centred around this. A boy is rejected if he is "unfaithful"—that is, if he goes out with another girl. The only positive action is to be "in circulation"—to go to parties and have plenty of opportunities to date. Girls with independence who play unusual roles are frowned upon, but if the girl is successful in getting her man she is allowed to have a few unconventional attitudes, although this is rare.

Friendship is interpreted in a negative way—a group of girls in an office who urge the heroine to get back into circulation is a common picture. Bad friends are those who are catty or say horrible things. Loyalty and deeper emotions of friendship are not involved. There is never any mention of religion, orthodox or otherwise. There is never any mention of violence apart from the odd story involving a motor-bike accident; drunkenness and smoking are not mentioned. The sub-culture seems to consist of office gossip, coffee drinking, parties and office parties.

Apart from the stock characters in the stories there are very few outsiders. In one story a "rich man" is involved because he befriends a young man whose dog he has knocked down, but not killed. He is pictured saying "Deah" and riding in a large car. Very few parents come into the stories. Occasionally there is a picture of a policeman who is walking his beat while the lovers are on their way home. There is the occasional appearance of an elder sister or friend who has stayed at school instead of getting a job. This ties in with the definite anti-intellectual bias. "Magic was in the air" is a short printed story by Liz Croft, published in *Jackie*. It was illustrated by a drawing of a very pretty girl, Anne, who described herself thus:

> I'm shy about liking poetry so much. It doesn't fit my face—I'm plain with glasses and ten thousand freckles.

In the story she explains why she is taking a solitary walk:

> There just hasn't been time for boy friends. Taking A levels means hours of study, and now that I am training to be a librarian, there seems to be even more to swot up.

In another story, Alison "can't help being a student teacher" and because she is a student, she has never "clicked" with boys. Studying is definitely equated with having no social life and not being available for constant dating.

Although the girls in the stories, almost without exception, work in offices, the boys have various jobs although they do not work in factories or do dirty work. Economics of living are not discussed. Girls appear to share flats or live at home, but this is rather vague and, except in special cases, parents do not intrude. Surroundings are always pleasant and modern-looking.

APPEARANCE

In the strip-stories girls have the same cast of face with tiny noses, huge eyes and very thick hair. Despite pouting lips and slim figures, they appear sexless; they are more like little girls dressed up than women. They always have long slim fingers and pretty, fashionable clothes.

The boys are tall, rugged and broad shouldered. They, too, have thick hair worn fairly long. They wear Carnaby Street clothes, but are boys rather than men.

The expressions are tailored to meet the needs of the stories. The characters are chirpy and gay, or sad with huge tears, meditative or blissfully happy. The men are easily recognisable as "shy" or "confident". "Wolves" are readily discernable. The boys and girls are either very blond or very dark. The expressions portrayed are completely straightforward. They illustrate immediately, with no subtlety, the feelings expressed and take the place of descriptive writing. In *Valentine* an unusual perspective is employed where there is a large figure or object in the foreground and small figures in the background like a series of stills from a film.

The artists who draw for *Jackie* go in for a more modern approach. The girls appear to be more fashionable. They wear up-to-the-minute clothes and are not as provincial as the girls in *Valentine*. *Jackie's* drawings are reminiscent of the new boutiques, but in *Valentine* they are realistic and have the flavour of the old Horlick's advertisements. The whole effect in *Jackie* is stark and not so detailed. *Jackie* carries a cartoon about a pop singer which is very similar to the strip-story drawings. The quality of the paper in *Jackie* and *Trend* is superior to that of *Valentine*. All the colour illustrations to the printed stories in *Jackie* and *Trend* are sentimental and more old-fashioned than the pictures for the strip-stories. Apparently all the blocks for *Jackie* come from Spain.

The drawings in *Trend* have a different technique. The girls are made to look young. They are like 12-year-old children with busts and 16-year-old dresses. The illustrations to the printed stories are poor, especially the illustrations to the romantic historical serial.

In the strip-story pictures of all three magazines the characters strike exaggerated poses which emphasise the situations in the stories. The drawings to the strip-stories in *Valentine* are less crude and the girls are startlingly pretty. The drawings are cruder in *Jackie* and *Trend* which, inevitably, makes the girls appear less attractive.

CHAPTER 3

Notes on pop music and the pop scene

You are always window shopping,
But never stopping to buy. . . .
(Words from "Georgie Girl", a current pop song)

APART from the articles, photographs and letters devoted exclusively to pop stars, their pictures appear on the fashion pages and, in one of the 3 magazines studied intensively, on the problem-letter page. The pop star dominates the teenage magazines as will be shown in the following study. The domination and, indeed, the whole rather mystical position of the pop star in popular culture today (1967) is interesting. Rapid improvement in broadcasting and recording techniques since the end of the last war have ensured a media of communication. Beginning in the late fifties the young wage-earner has had more money to spend than at any time in our history. This situation was exploited by the promoters and all concerned with commercial entertainment (the record business being one of the foremost).

The pop star could be virtually manufactured from raw material by a clever manager and sufficient plugging. His records (or those of his group) were released, plugged by the disc jockeys, articles were written about him and publicity developed around him. He was encouraged to wear "way-out" clothes and to buy "way-out" things. His image, rather than his musical talent, was implanted on the mind of the young person. The sense of identification was extremely strong, as the majority of young pop stars come from working-class homes.

The music itself, which has become so much a part of the teenage scene, cannot be defined easily. A short definition might be that it is a type of music primarily *aimed* at teenagers. A sizeable portion of pop is derived from jazz, and nowadays, especially, from the kind of jazz known as "Rhythm 'n Blues". The development of pop music and its adoption by the commercial world is given in Appendix I.

It is probably true to say that the kind of music and type of songs in vogue at a particular time are a reflection of the social mood of the time. The theme of the songs is almost always about some aspect of love. A year or so ago there was a spate of songs about boys getting killed on motor-cycles, but more often than not the words of the songs are completely trivial and banal. Unrequited love is a favourite:

> They say I'll love again some day
> True love will come my way
> The next time
> But after you there'll never be
> A next time
> For me

The superficiality ties up with the themes of the strip-stories in the teenage magazines. The newest and most sophisticated pop songs mention drugs and use drug jargon quite blatantly. There has been an extension of themes in the past year, which will be dealt with later in depth.

The musical side of pop is probably rather unimportant to the majority of fans, especially those who read pop gossip in the teenage magazines. What is important is that popsters can hum, sing or dance to the music itself: the music really seems to be a vehicle convenient for the expression and reception of the more significant aspects of pop—the psychological and sociological part. The word "pop" has only come into use since the Second World War and, with the host of associated words that have had their meanings devalued or altered, seems to reveal how well-organised commercially the pop industry is now. Along these lines pop could nowadays be defined as:

> The commercially aimed produce of a free-enterprising few in the form of a music based vehicle, presented to a dependable mass of people—mainly teenagers.

Once the response was estimated the supply was available.

Any number which gets into the Top Twenty published in the *Melody Maker* or the *Musical Express* is a pop song. The pirate radio stations, notably Radio London which has, at present, a vast listening audience especially among teenagers, consists entirely of commercially sponsored pop programmes. The type of programme originated with Radio Luxemburg which introduced the Top Twenty (the twenty best-selling pop records). Pirate radio stations have extended this to top thirties and top forties. The chart, as it is called, is a powerful influence in the pop business. The whole business itself has changed since the days when a singer or composer was auditioned in a musical publisher's office in Denmark Street. Apparently few of these offices contain even a piano nowadays. The unknown song writers and groups try to get hearings by the use of demonstration discs. Behind the screaming boy with his electric guitar are the back-stage men, the managers, agents, disc jockeys, pluggers and producers of pop TV shows. These highly professional and successful people are capable of giving the young teenager what he wants—or what he appears to want. He wants music which has an immediate impact on him.

The beat of pop music is strong and constant. It is simple, crude and compulsive. The instrumentation is built around this beat and the most prominent instrument is the electric guitar. Usually one guitar supplies melodic lines or harmonises the singer's melodic lines, and accompanying guitars are used rhythmically by striking one chord on each beat. Drums are always used to lay down the rhythmic base, and often the rhythm is further reinforced by bass or bass guitar and electronic organ which has now virtually superseded the piano. Thus each beat in the bar is emphasised by several instruments creating the driving rhythm.

The beat is emphasised in the gestures of the members of the group. The majority of pop musicians and singers cannot read music; in fact, promoters have said that real musical talent is often a handicap. On the whole, the musical content—the melodic structure, short progressions and rhythm—is elementary from a technical point of view.

Elvis Presley's first recordings were strong and sensual. He is quite a grandfather among pop stars, being over 30, but he still retains his popularity and has changed his appeal to fit in with current trends. The tender, ballad-like songs of Adam Faith and Cliff Richard still have a certain vogue, but the songs which The Beatles sing to thousands in Europe and America are not sex-motivated and have an almost innocent, family appeal. The latest recordings of The Beatles have become a little more tough and direct. At the peak of their popularity the flat Liverpudlian accent of The Beatles was the "in" voice, and the *Melody Maker* reported that many groups travel north to pick up authentic north-country accents. For years we have seen the idols of the entertainment world coming from America, and it is strange to note the tremendous success of The Beatles and other pop groups from England. In the January 1966 issue of the American magazine *Teen Screen*, which is a magazine devoted to information and gossip about pop stars, there is an article called "How to have an English accent: a Liverpool exclusive". For readers who might not be able to master the Liverpudlian vowels, there is a list of Liverpudlian expressions and English vocabulary which is the "in" language to use for American pop fans. Was it for their success in exporting flat Liverpudlian accents that The Beatles received their MBE's in 1965?

It is impossible to write of pop and pop stars without saying something about The Beatles who, 2 years ago, were mobbed in America as royalty and fashionable film stars have never been mobbed. Their fans, between the ages of 12 and 17, greeted them at London Airport when they took off or arrived from abroad. Special police had to control the mobs, and young people slept on the floors of the Airport waiting rooms so that they might catch a glimpse of The Beatles. This is true, but it is also true that the publicity men whipped up the enthusiasm and helped to create the mob hysteria which ensued. I was present at London Airport when a press photographer asked a group of young girls to lie on the floor of one of the lounges to be photographed. The girls had not, in fact, slept the night there. One had forced her way into our car at Hounslow West, the nearest tube station to the Airport. "You must take me to the Airport," she said, "you don't know what it means to me." No popularity could continue at such a peak, and the intensity has waned a little in the last 18 months, but the 4 young men are still very successful and their faces are as well known as those of the Queen or Sir Winston Churchill.

It has been remarked that when The Beatles have sung to live audiences not a word can be heard because of the screaming of the fans. It is noticeable that the screaming and hysteria increases when the young men sing in falsetto voices. A group called The Small Faces have just made a record which is practically all sung falsetto.

It is not my intention to develop the many aspects of pop music and its influence, but it is necessary to emphasise what a significant part it plays in teenage magazines. It also plays a big part in magazines designed for younger girls. *Princess, Diana, Judy, School Friend* and *Lady Penelope* are all popular with girls from the ages of 9 to 14, and this type of magazine has also become dominated by the pop scene.

Another aspect of the overall pop scene, of which the pop-dominated magazines are the foremost disseminators is "The Man from UNCLE", which began as a television show and is now the subject of feature films and paper-backed books. David McCallum is, perhaps, the magazines' favourite pin-up. Facts and pictures about him and Robert Vaughn, the stars, are constantly requested and supplied. The programme belongs to the current spy-film craze, and is also popular, perhaps, for regularly offering technical gadgets, burlesque and other features which popularise James Bond films. The series is also an exponent of the male glamour. The investigation of some worldwide plot builds up to the last-minute extrication from the near-fatal captivity of a standard adversary, THRUSH, and the frustration of its plot. Bond, similarly, is always opposed by SPECTRE or SMERSH, the Russian spy service. With their stream-lined division into acts and scenes, the ingenious equipment and the calm, wise-cracking facing of all danger by the investigators, these simple thrillers are specifically directed at a young audience. There is an immense sale of UNCLE goods, modelled usually on the gadgets from the show.

There has been a boom in folk music and protest songs during the past year. Six months ago Bob Dylan, an American folk singer who has had a big commercial success and can pack the Albert Hall, but who, nevertheless, sings songs about current events which are not in conformity with official American foreign policy, got into the English pop chart. Writing of him in *Jackie*, Pete's Private Eye said:

> I know that he sings songs about the stupidity of war and that his verses have great messages—and that's good. But what these folk fans mean by saying that Dylan is finished because people like you and me are buying his discs, I just don't know.
>
> If all these folk fans who worship Dylan and knock Donovan [an English commercial folk singer] were a bit less concerned with keeping their own way-out image, they would be pleased that these two artists are getting a lot of airplay and TV exposures. All of which is good for folk music in general. I think the folk boom is great. It's always good to have more people singing more songs. But let's not get too serious about the meaning of them.

The Monkees—Valentine, 4 March 1967

The Manfred Mann group have sung serious songs. One of their songs was featured in the *Daily Worker** because it was said to have been banned by the BBC. The song took the form of a letter to President Johnson about the war in Vietnam. The serious and protest songs are very few in comparison with the welter of songs which are completely superficial.

In the last year pop music has diversified in style, subjects and singers; new and revived styles compete, and no single sound dominates as the Liverpool sound once did. The Alan Price Set's "Simon Smith and his Amazing Dancing Bear" and the New Vaudeville Band's "Winchester Cathedral" are examples. Technical sophistication is shown in the orchestral accompaniments to the increasingly popular soloists such as Val Doonican, Petula Clark, Ken Dodd, Frank Sinatra and Jim Reeves. These stars are older and more removed from the pop scene, therefore their success appears to stem more from musical merit. Jim Reeves, a country and Western ballad singer, is more successful posthumously than when alive. He is an example of the cult of dead stars, such as Buddy Holly, Eddie Cochran and James Dean the film star. Their accidental deaths at the heights of their careers assured them of pop and film immortality. To the pop scene Jim Reeves is always "the late, great Jim Reeves" and his stereotyped, sad records are bought as a sentimental mourning.

Groups, too, now attend more to technical expertise, and the degree of musical innovation, particularly with regard to electronic distortion effects, as used on The Beatles' "Revolver" LP and also their latest singles, and by groups such as the Jimi Hendrix Experience, is a standard of success to fans.

The trend appears to improve and broaden pop music. A letter to the *Melody Maker* said:

> The excellence of the Beatles' latest single demonstrates their increasing ability to elevate the pop song to a more aesthetic and meaningful level.

Paul McCartney of The Beatles "wrote" a score for the film *The Family Way*, although, in fact, he cannot read music.

Connected with this trend is the lately more evident emergence of a pop élite, a fraternity at the centre of pop, whose interrelations and friendships fascinate fans. In music magazine terms they are "the stayers" and include groups such as The Beatles, The Rolling

* Now renamed *The Morning Star.*

Stones and The Hollies. Their individual names are well known and their status is now independent of the success of their current records. The letter written above by "Jazz pianist, Romford", went on to say:

> ... aided by inspired musicians and arrangers The Beatles are generating the "new situation" on the pop scene, which far from diminishing their popularity, will, I feel widen and perpetuate it.

Every week without fail the magazines mention these stars; at least one magazine gives them a regular feature: the national press, which counter to usual newspaper practice, covers them excessively, sees them as the pop world's representatives and of guaranteed interest; the popular Sunday press, denigrating or praising them according to the current pulse, also features them almost as a standard item in the same way as the fashion or political columns. They are members of British society's new aristocracy, celebrities in fashion, art, television, journalism and show business, not necessarily meritocrats, possibly just the fortunately picked example of a needed type "created" by publicity. The pop world is not yet represented in the Sociology textbook. The élite is a group of friends, as there are groups of friends centred on an office, a school or a club. Publicity projects them as the supreme example of this sort of thing.

These stars, perhaps personal friends, write songs for and attend one another's recording sessions. Part of the pop column in the *Melody Maker* gives an instance of this:

> One night they [Bob Dylan, and Brian Jones of the Rolling-stones] both tottered along at two o'clock in the morning to a recording studio with Wilson Pickett, and Brian and Bob got together on the words and the lads all cut a disc together.

The main difference between the élite and the less successful groups is that the former have a seeming indifference to modes of success. This may be calculated, but whatever they do becomes a new principle of success. While new groups use extreme versions of existing principles to make an impact, the élite appear to be above the need of obligation to fans; actual defiance further establishes them. Recently, on the ITV's "Sunday Night at the London Palladium" Sunday night show, The Rolling Stones refused to perform their latest single (which was the main reason for their appearance) without backing tapes, which, they claimed, would better reproduce the sound of their music.

This new élite are the champions of an esoteric morality and way of life, a "new consciousness", often sung about in songs such as "Tomorrow Never Knows" from the Beatles' LP "Revolver", "Let's Spend the Night Together" by The Rolling Stones, and Donovan's "Sunshine Superman". Part of the whole pop scene's basic self-deceiving cult of spontaneity and personality, this new outlook which might be called pop hedonism, is an intellectualisation by older, richer, more articulate stars of existing pop values, with emphasis on the spontaneous, individual, unconventional, random, their type of the artistic (a sort of surrealism), and on the absence of a normal routine. There is emphasis on the wider indulgence of the senses as possibly provided by the drug LSD which is regarded as a creative stimulant.* Unlike their fans the élite pop stars are financially able to make day-trips across the Atlantic and to hire 60-guinea boxes at opera premieres.

Graham Nash, of The Hollies, said in an interview:

> The influential groups and stars are more interested in playing better pop music and educating younger people about the good, beautiful things in life.

Nash was said to be stating: " . . . the new pop philosophy that emanates from some of pop's biggest stars."

Nash went on about the influence of pop:

> I feel it's just teaching. It's part of life. I just dig imparting knowledge of love and beautiful things that you're just not going to learn about in school. Young people are in a very beautiful position. Their minds are still open and usually pure. They haven't matured and they haven't yet been *pressured* by society, custom and tradition to think a certain way about certain things . . . Unfortunately much of life is such that most kids begin to get screwed up inside by fifteen. Maybe good sincere pop music can just show these people that freedom does exist. I want more people to dig everything that's going on around them . . . records have almost taken the place of newspapers. . . .
>
> Look at the Beatles. They are a classic example of a group that stimulates other people. . . .

* This was the first reflection in the English pop movement of a long-standing trend in America which originated in San Francisco—The Hippies, Beautiful People or The Flower Children.

... Man, if fourteen-year olds could do what the Beatles are doing now that would be beautiful.

In an interview quoted in the *Melody Maker* Donovan said:

I'm very excited, though, by the acceptance of songs like "Eleanor Rigby" [a Beatles hit]. It proves that though kids won't read so many books any more, they'll listen to a novel in a song.

Fans have always looked for the relationship between the personal lives of stars and the song lyrics. Now stars are explicitly stating their views on life and values.

Electronic effects are a feature of the more serious pop music—a "psychedelic" (mind-expanding) result which is a form of musical surrealism indicated in The Beatles' "Strawberry Fields Forever". Some songs refer to drugs or try to simulate the sound effects of drugged states. The *News of the World*, in February 1967, published a series of intensive articles on the connection between drugs and the pop world.

One of the articles began:

It is impossible to exaggerate the hold which the halucination drug LSD has gained on the pop world during the past year, or the speed with which it is becoming "fashionable" among the beat groups teenage fans.

It went on to say:

Some record companies are cracking down on psychedelic songs. For instance, EMI several times revised this week's release "My Friend Jack" by a group called The Smoke.

They rejected the first title "My Friend Jack eats Sugar Lumps" because of its obvious LSD suggestions.

The chorus of The Move's first hit, "Night of Fear", contained:

Just about to flip your mind;
Just about to *trip* your mind.

("Trip" is the term for the influence of LSD.) "I Can Hear the Grass Grow" represents an impression purportedly possible under LSD. Donovan's LP "Fairy Tale" contains "Sunny Goodge Street" which begins:

On the fire-fly platform
On Sunny Goudge Street
A violent hash smoker shook a chocolate machine. ...

The Cream—Jackie, 4 March 1967

Writing of Donovan the *News of the World* said:

> Our investigation has shown that drugs have played a part in Donovan's day-to-day life and in the songs he writes too.
>
> On the B side of "Sun-shine Superman" is a record entitled "The Trip".
>
> The song describes how Donovan and a friend lock themselves up before going to sleep. . . . How a "driver" appears and takes them off on a trip in which they live their halucinatory dreams.
>
> He sings about his "dream Woman" and halucination who has sequins in her hair and sits on a white chair.
>
> As the singer sits and watches the whole scene bursts like a bubble before him—entirely consistent with a "happening" under LSD. Donovan then talks to the girl and asks her to take a trip and join him.
>
> Of course to the uninitiated the words are difficult to follow.

It is doubtful how much of the true meaning of these drug-based records is understood by younger and less sophisticated fans.

Connected with these songs is "freak-out"—extreme electronic music, possibly part of a "happening", an organised "spontaneous" group reaction of self-expression typified by "The Who's" ending a performance with the breaking of their instruments and equipment, or "The Move" smashing up objects. A record called "Freak-out" oy The Mothers of Invention was reviewed in the *Melody Maker*:

> Throwing off their social chains, freeing themselves from their national social slavery and realising what potential they possess for free expression, The Mothers of Invention toss the moral code aside like spare sugar lumps [LSD is often taken absorbed by sugar lumps]. That is, they're sending up American society, advocating free love, nay advocating freedom already. The medium they have chosen is mainly electronics, echo, the occasional feeding back guitars, thundering drums. Vocally you are presented with a studio full of "freaks" looning about and reminding you that they can give you motherly love 'till you don't know what to do.

This whole trend is linked with Op and Pop-art and the "beat" movement. It shows stars accepting a role as instigators of ideas and values as well as fashion trends for profit.

The élite is established and maintained by publicity exemplified by the confidential tit-bits in the inside pop columns which pretend the existence of a swinging scene with the appeal of exclusiveness.

Trend says:

> Disappointed to hear that Proby's visit to Britain was off. It isn't the same in the in-clubs these days without our Jim looning about. And there are so many dollies who feel the same way.

Such is the social circle to which teenage magazines induce readers to aspire, just as pop success, its travelling, fame and riches, is the present symbol to youth of making one's fortune. The globe-trotting, which stars emphasise, is, too, a symbol of independence and removal from routine of which fans under parental control dream. The teenage magazines tone down the more unconventional antics of the pop stars to a stream of rather dreary trivia.

Pop entertainment is expanding and films in a particular style of burlesque and varied camera effects, such as The Beatles' "Help" are released with groups as stars. Similar films, featuring the stars, accompany the playing of records on "Top of the Pops". A situation comedy TV show starring a new group, The Monkees, is in similar style. This group and their swift success is a supreme example of stars created by publicity. They were picked as actors for the show in which the gang's adventures form an ideal pop life. The Monkees' records and show have boosted one another's popularity. The fierce argument about them among fans, their relation to The Beatles and prepared success, shows how seriously pop is regarded; there are hostile factions just as in politics. The music papers have always regarded pop as an art form. They have a technical criticism for reviews; they refer to genres, "soul", "R and B", "C and W", "rock", "Tamla Motown", "folk", "ballad", "freak-out", "Atlantic-tinged numbers".

Another change in pop entertainment is the extension and revision of the BBC Light Programme's pop show "Easy Beat" on Sunday morning along the lines of pirate radio shows. It now contains zany humour, strange sound effects and listeners' letters. All these innovations offer more explicit standards of behaviour, conversation, outlook and dress.

It is almost impossible to separate pop *music* from the whole pop scene. Just as pop has invaded the romantic and juvenile magazines, so it appears to be the crux on which the lives of many young people centre. Their clothes, hair styles, speech and attitudes are all a reflection of the pop scene. Pop music is unquestionably necessary to modern youth, but is this necessity a compulsive force which has been thrust upon them, or has it made lives richer which were relatively empty before? Pop music could be considered one of the lowest forms of art, having a mass appeal culture in the same vein as the television serials "Coronation Street" or "Emergency Ward Ten". Does the fact that its appeal is immediate, direct and emotionally immature help it to attract an age group which is itself emotionally and mentally unformed?

It is true that in addition to the enormous sales of pop records, classical recordings and recordings in general have risen since the war. There are very few young people who do not escape altogether the appeal of pop music. This is understandable as anyone born into the present younger generation could hardly fail to respond, at some time or another, to the compulsive rhythms and tuneful melodies of contemporary pop music. The following passage written by a young polytechnic student, himself a good pianist of modern jazz, may help to explain the relationship between pop music and the particular kind of dancing it inspires:

> The wild jerking and twitching which older people cannot comprehend as the dancing, which some pop music evokes in today's youngsters is, in fact, a very natural basic expression, uncontrived or conditioned, but simply free and uninhibited, and this sort of expression of oneself in whatever form never did anybody any harm. In fact, it is positively a good thing if kept within bounds, where it is harmless to others, although, unfortunately, this is not always the case. These modern dances are often compared with those of African natives and tribal rituals etc. Well, there is a very low incidence of neuroticism amongst African tribes. These instinctively felt, often blatantly sexual movements could be simply interpreted as a direct reaction against our sophisticated, contrived and wayward society which has unwittingly been one of the main instigators of this powerfully influential form of music.

CHAPTER 4

The image of the pop star

The very presumptuousness of moulding or affecting the human mind through the techniques we use has created a deep sense of uneasiness in our minds.

(W. HOWARD CHASE, President, Public Relations Society of America, 1956)

MORE than 50 per cent of the material printed in teenage magazines is devoted to pictures of and features about the current pop stars. The features range from large photographs with full-length articles to tit-bits with or without small pictures of the stars. Few of the current pop stars are girls. In the main the stars are groups of boys, and the group has a name such as The Beatles, The Rolling Stones, The Who, The Animals, The Small Faces, The Walker Brothers, The Rockin' Berries, The Peeps, The Hollies, The Ygrades, The Applejacks, The Beatstalkers, The Chasers, The Bachelors, The Searchers, The Dave Clark Five, The Spencer Davis Group, The Rattles, The Eyes, The Shots, The Righteous Brothers, Herman's Hermits, The Mindbenders, The Tremeloes, The Dakotas, The Byrds, The Monkees, Dave Dee, Dozy, Beaky, Mick and Tich, The Troggs, The Four Tops and The Beach Boys.

Some of these groups never appear in London but play in the provinces the whole time. They all compete to get into the Top Twenty which is published every week. The top ten records, which are those with the biggest sales and the most popular acclaim, guarantee success for the groups or individuals. The television, radio programmes and pirate stations featuring the successful pop songs achieve enormous popularity, as is shown by the figures taken from the questionnaires in Chapter 7.

Interest in the minor groups is sustained by the features and pieces of information in the teenage magazines. *Valentine* has two full pages of letters from readers asking for information about the groups. Here are a few samples:

Q. "I bet you can't tell me how much Val Doonican's little baby daughter weighed at birth." Christine Liversedge (Walsall)

A. "Sorry you lose, Christine. Little Sarah Louise weighed 8 lb. 10 oz."

Q. "What colour eyes has deejay Pete Brady?" Ann Craddock (Ruislip).

A. "Pete has grey/blue peepers."

Q. "Please could you tell me which of The Stones weighs the least?" Judy Clifford (Amersham).

A. "Two Stones share this honour—Keith Richard and Bill Wyman at 10 st. each."

Asking the weight, the colour of eyes and hair, the hobbies, the size in shoes and such pieces of trivial information come up regularly in the letters. A fair proportion ask for definite information on the instruments played by members of the group, the numbers recorded on the flip-side (song recorded on the other side of the record playing a very popular number) of records, and the number in the chart which a record has reached.

It is difficult to decide whether the magazines are parasites on the pop star industry or vice versa. The character and slant of the magazines would be entirely different without the pop star pictures and features. *Valentine* carries a double-page spread purported to be written by The Beatles. Each week it has a picture of this most famous group who answer readers' letters. Here are a few random letters with their answers:

DEAR RINGO,
What will happen when we run out of questions to ask you?
JULIE BAILY (Sherwood, Nottingham).
Ringo replies:

Then you can start asking us answers and we'll tell you what questions we think go with them.

DEAR FANTABULOUS GEORGE,
This is the thirteenth time I have written to you, but my letters never seem to get through. I read in a book that you are blunt and outspoken. Is this true?
JANET (Twickenham).

George answers:

> Blunt? Outspoken? I dunno really Janet, but if that means saying what you really think, then I suppose I am.

> DEAR FAB BEATLES,
> Was the lion that nearly attacked Ringo in *Help* a real one or a stuffed one?
>> ANNE STEWART (Cardenden, Fife, Scotland).
>> (*Help* was a film featuring The Beatles)

John replies:

> I'd better answer this for Ringo or you might think he was kidding. That lion was a TIGER, Anne, but it was certainly real enough, believe me!

Ringo comments:

> That tiger was also stuffed mate. You should have seen the amount of raw meat it stuffed away when we had a lunch break!

> DEAR RINGO,
> Is it true that you are going to send Zak to Eton?
>> A FAN WHO ADORES *Help* (Croft Road,
>> Yardley, Birmingham 26).
>> (Zak is Ringo's baby son.)

Ringo replies:

> Definitely untrue! I don't think we would want Zak to go to any type of boarding school and we both want him to have an ordinary uncomplicated education.

Week after week the letters appear, asking for the size of Ringo's shoes, the colour of Paul's pyjamas as well as minute details about making discs and trivial incidents which happened at one-night stands. Apparently the editors have so many letters that they can barely read them.

Trend publishes fewer letters about pop stars, but they are of the same calibre:

> DEAR PAT,
> I have been wanting to send up and ask you because it has been bothering me for a long time why Steve Marriott of The Small Faces

sticks his finger in his earhole when he sings up high. He always does it. Is there something wrong with his ear or is it just habit?

SUSAN WALKER (262 Feltham Hill Road,
Ashford, Middx.)

Pat replies:

Steve says he sings like this because when he is in a large hall, and the mikes are so loud, he can't hear if he's on key. He said, "You should try sticking your finger in your ear when you are talking".

The many features on the individual pop stars of the various groups aim to give a picture of young men who are, in the main, typical of any secondary modern boy but who have a certain amount of glamour and are allowed a few eccentricities within a limited range. They are often described as "interesting" and "controversial", but when analysed this often means just an ability to indulge in something beyond the reach of the ordinary working boy of the same age. A typical example is the very successful Dave Clark, leader of the firmly established The Dave Clark Five, who has recently bought a £25,000 house for his parents. He tells how he went to the family flat over a grocer's shop in Tottenham and told his parents to choose a house which he would buy. He devised the interior decoration himself:

The decor is off-beat, a black ceiling and shaded red lights in the lounge . . . warm splashes of orange, turquoise and magenta in the bedrooms . . . and gleaming brass all over the place, hunting horses, muskets with brass facings, miniature cannon, bowls and jugs, horse-brasses galore.

When asked about his plans for a house should he marry, Dave Clark replied:

If I married I would move. I would get a house right in the country with 20 acres of grounds and a stable of horses and lots of dogs. Maybe that is looking ahead and dreaming a bit—but if you didn't look ahead and dream, life would be a lot poorer, don't you reckon?

As the magazines are composed almost exclusively of strip-stories and feature articles on pop stars, it is interesting to note that pop stars are allowed their cars and houses and £50 a week "sweet" money (The Who), while the girls and boys in the strip-stories have very modest expectations. Both, however, are allowed to dream.

Mike (Michael Smith) who is the pianist in the Dave Clark Five says: "I'm a normal boy from a working-class home with the best parents anyone could have."

Mike Smith was born in 1943 and educated at Montague Secondary Modern School, North London. He normally pays £35 for a jacket, £12 for slacks and £8 each for hand-made shirts. He says that he "digs sailing and speed-boating, wearing a beret to keep sun from his eyes. He likes tea so much, he once ordered a pot for three—just for himself."

Keith Richards (one of The Stones), another pop star who writes or purports to write a column for *Trend* says:

> I'm never one for expressing myself in words. My Mum gets dead grotty because I don't send her great fat letters when I go away. She pulls a face when I send her a postcard with a skyscraper on, and Love Keith on it. . . . We all bought [in America] suits and jackets and new gear for our wardrobes. I suppose you think it must be a bit dull buying clothes so often. But, you know, it isn't. In fact, sometimes just being able to buy something, gives me a great kick.

Donovan, a singer of protest songs who appears to be strongly influenced by the American folk singer Bob Dylan, writes about his interest in clothes:

> I'm always on the look-out for clothes in tangerine. It's my fave colour, but you don't often see clothes that colour. So I have to have a special search around Carnaby Street, or keep a watch on all the men's shops in the provinces when I'm driving through—and if I see something in tangerine. I nip out for a closer look and maybe buy it.

Jim of The Honour collects socks. Readers are asked to get knitting: any colour or pattern.

Again, in a feature article about a group called The Who, the four young men are presented as being "different":

> They are experts in such varying things as Superman magazine (they read them), clothes (they make them), free speech (they practise it).
> "We do what we want," they said firmly, "we don't care if it's the thing to read books—we like magazines."

Roger Daltrey, the singer of the group, said he made a sweater:

> It's got a polo neck on which I've stuck black felt stripes. I've got a belt I covered in black sellotape to go with it! There's no end to what you can make on the spot.

Peter Townsend, the guitarist, is especially interested in experimenting with pop art. He described how he bought himself:

> . . . a white Levi jacket and a white linen jacket, too. The first I treated with wads of cotton wool dipped in different kinds of dye, and the result was a great rainbow effect. The linen jacket I dipped in peacock green dye, but just momentarily, then squeezed it through and the result was a highly successful mottled look.

The Who, who have become very successful during the past year, have always aimed to be controversial and different. Peter Townsend stresses how they do not spend their spare time together:

> We hate each other quietly. We never go around together after work, be a drag we reckon. We've got our own manors, so we don't hang about together. Roger's manor is Shepherd's Bush where he is king among mods. I drive this fast Jag, wear cool clothes, give them the works.

Wearing rather unusual clothes and not going about together in non-working hours is taken as evidence of the daring attitudes of these young men. They do, however, express their opinions in the following song which became a hit number, and is called rather significantly "My Generation":

> People try to put us down,
> (Talking 'bout my generation)
> Just because we get around
> (Talking 'bout my generation)
> Things they do look awful cold
> (Talking 'bout my generation)
> Hope I die before I get old
> (Talking 'bout my generation).

Interviewed in *Trend*, Pete Townsend said about the song:

> This number was written ages ago, immediately after "Can't Explain"—The Who's first record. It is definitely not a protest

song. In actual fact we think this protest stuff is rubbish. We've been doing a bit of protest against protest, wearing shirts with BAN PROTEST written on them, on TV programmes and stuff like that, sending it all up. Personally, I don't think protest has a place in commercial music. Some of the protest songs which have been done by smaller folk groups are laughable.

Pete Townsend was asked: "Is there any message in this number then?"

No, there's no message really. It's a song about feelings. "I can't Explain" was a song about love. "Anyway, Anyhow, Anywhere" was about a young bloke who was cocky and thought he could do anything he wanted. "My Generation", I suppose, is a slightly nostalgic song.

It reminds us of the days before the Mod thing started dwindling. The time when there was this feeling in the air, when you ran down the streets without any responsibilities and got stoned out of your mind, and smashed windows. You see, now all the Mods are getting older [explained Peter].

I'm twenty, and most of the fellas who were in my year at school have stopped being Mods and have joined the Army or got jobs in factories or things like that.

Then there's the stammering on the record, which is a way of demonstrating the inability of young people to express themselves.

The words of "My Generation" express a completely negative outlook. There is an antagonism towards growing old which is expressed overtly here, and underlies much of the attitude in the strip-stories and in other pop songs. The second verse of "My Generation" is:

> Why don't you all fade away
> (Talking 'bout my generation)
> Don't try and dig what we all say,
> (Talking 'bout my generation).

The only positive value expressed is the insular world of the young as opposed to the "other" world of older people. Older people never understand, they are outside, they cannot have fun and are completely divorced from the teenage life. To grow old is a crime. This is evident from the strip-stories in the magazines, because the stories always finish when the romance is settled. Marriage, responsibility, getting older are developments with which "my generation" does not concern itself.

John Lennon of The Beatles, one of the more articulate of the pop singers, is quite open about his fear of growing old. "The thing I'm afraid of is growing old and you've missed it somehow."

Could this be a result of having a generation of parents who "missed it" somehow during the Second World War?

The following quizz game which was taken from *Jackie* is interesting because it defines "being old".

"Do you think that being old (that is, over 35) must be:

(a)   All right when you get there?
(b)   Dreadful and boring and ugly?
(c)   Very comforting and secure?
(d)   More of a challenge?

The present-day pop star is fully aware of the cult of the anti-hero, and many of these young men stress their feelings of fear and insecurity. *Jackie* printed a full-page chart asking five pop stars and TV star David McCallum about their likes and dislikes. One question was about childhood fears. With one exception all the young men mentioned insecurity, being frightened and having fears. When interviewed many pop stars make a play of insecurity and retention of childhood fears.

Alan Price, described in *Trend* as "a serious young man who finds success worrying", said:

I must admit, I am a neurotic. (He turned his attention to a newspaper which he ripped thoughtfully and continued).

People were saying I was neurotic for years, but I have only just accepted the fact. This was my real reason for leaving The Animals.

Reading through the features article on pop stars one is struck by a recurring theme: that of buying things. This is reinforced in other features in the magazines. Happiness is frequently equated with spending money. The Editor of *Trend* says:

If you fancy more clothes to keep you happy—then take a peek at our super colour spread on bright, bright needlecords.

The excellent anti-smoking advertisements show a girl surrounded by all the things she has bought as a result of giving up smoking. Every week readers are told what current pop stars buy:

Keith of The Seekers was in Bournemouth last summer working in the summer season. There he did a lot of water-ski work. He is thinking seriously of buying a powerful boat.

While Bruce Woodley of The Seekers said:

I'm going to change my Jag soon. Working so much around London you don't get too much chance to let her rip.

Many of the young men appear to be highly interested in the accessories to fashion which, at one time, were considered to be confined to a girl's province. An article in *Trend* reveals that:

The first thing you notice about twenty-four year old Steve Darbishire, Singer, is the ear-ring he wears pierced through his left ear.
When I was fifteen I met this French Bohemian girl. We fell madly in love, but neither of our families approved. So instead of getting engaged, she bought a pair of ear-rings and we had one each!
Now he doesn't know where she is anymore, but whenever he falls for a new girl, he proposes the idea of wearing his ear-ring!
Steve has some original fashion ideas, which he wears himself, like an Indian metal clip instead of a tie, and trousers so hipster that he calls them thighsters!

Sonny and Cher are two American popular singers who have achieved great popularity in the States and this country. They are married and *Trend* gave them a two-page spread with pictures of their large expensive house in California. They are described thus:

She's the most knock-out bird that ever flew the Atlantic and hubby's a gas as well. They're a space-age couple. They're like a delicious giant-size box of liquorice all-sorts to watch.
Smaller, ultra male with almost a trace of the hip young caveman about him, that's Sonny. She, with her over-emphasised make-up, beautiful, rich-coloured hair and way-ahead clothes. In their case married life is like a fabulous, eccentric ballet full of fun.

The article goes on to say how their life is not a dull, ordinary married life where she stays at home and waits for him to come in from work. Cher has a man who:

. . . walks around barefoot and loves brushing her hair and giving her new ideas for a wardrobe that springs up like a never-dying bed of exotic flowers. They can even fit snugly into each others skin-tight jeans and sweaters, if they want.

You think that marriage curbs freedom and turns into a habit too soon? This type of marriage looks like proving just the opposite. How could you help making your stage act the greatest when it's the dolliest bird you know that you're singing alongside, or those eyes you're grinning into belong to your knight in zany mod gear? And they sang, and lived happily ever after.

If the *Trend* reader marries her boy next door and they start looking for somewhere to live in Britain of 1967 she is going to be rather disappointed if she has been identifying herself with Cher Bono.

Although almost all the young pop stars have a strong sense of identification and appear to come from similar backgrounds to the readers of the teenage magazines, a small number are outside this range. In January 1966 a young man from Swansea called Spencer Davis became the first graduate of a British University (Birmingham) to get to the top of the hit parade.

Mr. Davis took a second in German in 1963, and in 1966 his record "Keep on Running" replaced The Beatles as number 1 in the charts. Three other pop stars, Peter Asher, Mike Sarne and Mick Jagger, were all at London University and Paul Jones of the Manfred Mann group was at Oxford, but none of these took his degree. These young men are exceptions. The identification angle is exploited to its full extent. Again and again readers of teenage magazines are assured that the pop stars are just ordinary boys from ordinary homes. The features and gossip items follow a set pattern. After the introduction of identification, the pop star demonstrates his "way-out" dress and "way-out" habits as indicated in the quotations. The words "dreams" and "dreamland" occur frequently, and it is the exploitation of the dreams of teenagers which is so profitable to the business men behind the teenage magazines and the record industry.

Almost all pop stars, when featured in articles describe their wardrobes, houses, cars and "controversial" tastes or habits. These are mentioned more often than the actual music or songs. An article on The Kinks says:

> Dave Davies is in action, bombing around London in his new red Mini car, scaring pedestrians and motorists out of their lives with honks on his hooter and screeches from his tyres.

Another member of the group is described thus:

> Ray's in action too. He's moved house and bought a place in Finchley. A big mod pad with a spiral staircase and 12 rooms.

Although the biggest support for pop stars comes from girls, the stars themselves are not portrayed as having a great interest in the other sex. *Valentine* has an article about The Chasers:

> Clothes-wise the most colourful and mod group around is The Chasers who debutted with "Hey Little Girl". They are Carnaby Street's delight. On being questioned about likes and dislikes they all said: "We all go for mod way-out hipster, outlandish gear."

On being quizzed about girls only three of the five put girls in their list of likes. The other two went for cars and composing songs.

A high proportion of the pop gossip about stars is devoted to clothes. The following extract is a typical example:

> Jonathan King tells me he is already planning a new look for men next summer. It is called the Check Look. Jonathan, you see, digs wearing things with a mesh design—and got this Check Look idea through a string vest. . . . "I came back very late from a TV show and was so tired that I simply put my pyjama jacket on without bothering to take off my string vest. Next morning I found I had a real way-out design imprinted on the top part of my body. I then figured that if you sunbathed wearing a string vest you could get a fantastick Check Look for the beach that would catch the girls—yes, double fast."

One can read thousands of words about the likes and dislikes, habits and way-out ideas of the boys in the pop groups and have no idea about their music. Here is a typical item about a group:

> Most groups get pretty bored hanging about in their dressing rooms before they go on stage, whilst they are on tour—but The Small Faces have solved this.
>
> They have been buying up vast quantities of little mechanical robots—and now stage battles across the dressing room floor.
>
> According to them it's a good way of passing time.

The buyers of records must be interested in the music, but certainly, in the teenage magazines most of what is written about groups and individual singers is in the form of tit-bits, which takes us back to the days of George Newnes. The "controversial" and "way-out" habits of pop stars appear to be concentrated on wearing and part-making original clothes and enlargement of personal habits. The trivial likes and dislikes of the young men are written about each week, and the "controversial" or "different" angle is strained to the limits of banality, as in the following:

> Mad about mushrooms—that's Mick Tinsley, lead singer with Hedgehoppers Anonymous. "I could eat 'em four times a day," Mick tells me. "Bacon and mushrooms for breakfast; steak and mushrooms for lunch; mushrooms on toast for tea; mushroom pie at night."
>
> When The Hedgehoppers go driving around, Mick takes a small wicker basket in the car. "If I see a likely spot in the country," he says, "I insist on stopping the car—getting out—and collecting my mushrooms a hundred per cent fresh."

Romances, such as those between Mick Jagger (The Rolling Stones) and Marianne Faithful and Chrissie Shrimpton (the model Jean Shrimpton's sister), or between Paul McCartney and the actress Jane Asher, are public. Of Marianne Faithful *Disc* said:

> Everyone's talking about the new-look Marianne Faithful. Once she was dainty and delicate, sang like a shivering nightingale and lived utterly in accord with what one might expect of a convent-educated daughter of a baroness.
>
> And now? She's hip . . . swing . . . wears amazing colour combines and clothes styles. She wears huge, floppy ties and large baggy trousers. She even turns up at important Covent Garden occasions with absolute disregard for protocol by arriving after Royalty have taken their seats. . . .
>
> . . . once the non-showbiz mother. . . .
>
> . . . and now? Estranged from her husband she's back . . . a new romance with pop's most eligible Mick Jagger. His clothes sense has a lot to do with the way she is dressing now. . . .

It would be easy to be scornful of the trivial nature of the pop gossip which is poured out week after week, but it is no worse than the plethora of "human interest" tit-bits and stories which are churned out day after day and week after week in our popular daily and Sunday newspapers. The main difference seems to be that the pop stars pad their gossip items with clothes news. Dress for the teenagers has become a minor cult. It is also an identifying factor. Some years after the war, groups of working-class boys in south London started the Teddy Boy Fashion. They copied and exaggerated the Edwardian styles wearing long jackets, velvet collars, key chains and thick soled shoes. Their suits were made to

c

measure and often cost them the equivalent of two or three weeks' wages. The girls who accompanied them wore rather severe tailor-made skirts and jackets.

The rejection of conventional clothes made many adults equate Teddy Boys with violence and delinquency, and the word Teddy Boy, although it is now very dated, is often used to mean a boy who is a hooligan and has been in trouble with the police. The Teddy Boy fashion in clothes did not survive, and one of the main reasons must have been that it was not possible for the mass-market in clothes to enter into the field of tailor-made suits. The teenager today, and particularly the young pop singer who is seeking attention, may alter and add to his clothes, but he seldom has them made by a tailor. When the Mods v. Rockers disputes were taking place in 1963 I asked many boys and girls what was the difference between the two sets and most of them gave the answer: different clothes and different music.

A study of teenage magazines shows that in the strip-stories the clothes, while modern, are not "way-out", but the pop gossip is about 60 per cent concerned with the clothes of the young men. The segregation between clothes for the teenager and clothes for his relatively young parents is sharp. The Teddy Boys copied the dress of the well-off Edwardian, but the teenager today rejects the smart, but in their eyes, "dowdy" clothes of the rich of today. It is always a shock to see or hear an interview with a young pop star who is making his way and is dressed in his own particular style. He can express himself in his music and his clothes, but usually he fails to express himself verbally. The most caustic comments were passed in the press about a television programme starring Donovan, a famous pop singer, who was reported to have said that "beauty is a beautiful thing". He is one of the more articulate pop singers.

The need to express oneself through what one wears has become a powerful factor in the lives of young people. Naturally it is com-mercialised because changing fashion, for instance, in such matters as bell bottoms replacing narrow-trousered jeans, means that new clothes are bought and others discarded. Despite the prevalence of young men with long hair, beards and casual clothes, and girls with long hair and "kinky" clothes, there is a hostility by a large proportion of adults towards this type of appearance. This is fostered in the teenage magazines, and segregation between teen-agers and adults is brought into play.

CHAPTER 5

Other Items

PART I. FASHION AND ILLUSTRATIONS

There is a definite demarcation between the clothes as worn by the characters in the strip-stories and the fashion drawings. The fashion illustrations in *Jackie* and *Trend* are smart and up to date, in fact they set the trend for what young girls would like to wear in the same way as the pop stars like to set trends for their clothes. They emphasise fashions which are "way-out" and almost *avant-garde*. Some of the fashion articles give advice on dyeing clothes and making accessories. This links up with the clothes gossip put out about The Who, one of the most successful groups of the moment. The articles in all three magazines are realistic about prices and budgeting.

The fashions in *Jackie* and *Trend* tend to be particularly modern, but *Trend* caters for a slightly older age group. (*Trend* now carries no strip-stories and is becoming more and more like a young girl's fashion magazine and less like a strip-story comic.) The fashion drawings in *Jackie* are striking, and emphasise the attitude of the younger girl who wants to be completely up to the minute and to "shock" rather than to "appeal". The current vogue for very short skirts is accentuated by drawings of girls with extremely long legs and practically no skirt at all. They appear to be caricatures of top models, with perfectly symmetrical faces, enormous eyes and heart-shaped mouths with tiny snub noses. They have long, thin necks, square shoulders and emaciated figures. They have the almost perverse appeal of an innocent child dressed in bizarre, sophisticated clothes.

The fashion drawings in *Valentine* occupy less space and are not an important part of the magazine. The articles are rather ordinary but give good advice on buying reasonably priced clothes available

55

in most of the small chain stores which cater mainly for young working girls. In contrast, the girls in the strip-stories are shown in more fashionable clothes; in particular they wear more formal party dresses, which seem slightly old-fashioned for today's teenagers.

In the strip-stories in *Jackie*, the faces especially the girls' hair styles, seem to take precedence over the fashions. One is aware that the girl is young, pretty and reasonably fashionably dressed from the first picture, and she can be more easily identified with the reader than the exaggerated fashion model.

PART II. LETTERS

Am not I happy that amidst all these glooms
I can sit in my closet and write to you.
   (Letter to the Earl of Chesterfield from the Lady R., 1672)

Over 1200 children between the ages of 11 and 18 answered a questionnaire on reading comics and magazines, and an average of 25 per cent of them said they would like to see more letters to the Editor. *Jackie*, *Trend* and *Valentine* all cater for this taste. The "problem" letters in *Valentine* represent 4 per cent of the total output of the magazine; in *Trend* the "problem" letters represent 3 per cent. In *Jackie* the percentage is 5, but the letters are partly humorous and some of those printed receive a prize.

An analysis of the problems involved which is substantiated by the experience of a reporter working on one of these magazines shows that the greatest number of queries concern:

(a) Getting a boy friend.
(b) Worry about over-weight, spotty complexion, wearing glasses or some aspect of unsatisfactory appearance.
(c) Difficulties about losing a boy friend, or complications arising when a romance is not working out.
(d) Conflicts with parents.

According to authentic information every reader who writes to *Jackie* receives a duplicated reply. The replies are prepared and duplicated to fit the stock situations. Each letter ends with a message of goodwill and encouragement to the reader to continue reading the magazine. The letters which are printed are answered by Samantha, and £2 is given for the best letter and £1 each for the

Broadway—Jackie, 1 July 1967

The Stay-At-Home Hair Salon

Do-it-yourself styles for girls who want a head start

by Beauty Editor Terry Anderson

Do-it-yourself hair style—Trend, 15 April 1967

next two best. Many of the letters describe humorous situations. The quality of the letters may be judged from the following award winning letter:

He wants her to give him a perm.

We often hear boys complain about how much we girls fuss with our hair, but my boy friend is the limit.

On our first date he asked me to excuse the state of his hair (which looked perfectly O.K. to me). He had just washed it and his back-combing would not stay in. Of course, I took it as a joke then, but now I believe it.

He can't go out with me on two nights a week. These are kept sacred for hair washing. He's often confessed to using his mother's hair lacquer and he's now even trying to persuade me to give him a light perm.

JACKY JONES (Abergavenny, Mon.)

The problem letters printed in *Trend* are answered by Secretary Sally and an advisory panel which consists of a psychologist, a fashion and beauty editress, and a guest, who is always a pop star. The letters printed in this magazine are more serious and do reveal a glimpse of real problems. The two following letters are quoted because they involve concern with educational and speech deficiencies. There was scope here for comprehensive answers offering real guidance to the writers, but it was not given. The first letter deals with difficulties in English and writing letters:

DEAR SALLY,

I was never very bright at school since I hated anything to do with learning, but I have got a good job in a shop and a wonderful boy friend. The trouble is he's going away for three months on a job and wants me to write to him every day. The thought petrifies me, as I have always found it difficult to put my thoughts into words—and I'm a rotten speller too. My sister has offered to write the letters for me, and I am wondering if I should accept her offer.

SUSAN (Doncaster)

Sally answers:

Your boy friend wants to hear from YOU, and your sister, no matter how much she tried, could never copy your style. Even if you dictate a letter to her I'm pretty sure you would get self-conscious about saying what you really want to say.

The psychologist advised Susan to think out loud and put down her thoughts on paper. This is reasonably helpful, but there was scope here for a genuinely constructive answer. No one advised Susan to use a dictionary or attend an evening class in English.

Another reader on the same page says that her boy friend speaks badly and it irritates her. She wants advice on how to help him without annoying him. Sally advises the reader to say to her boy friend that it is a pity he speaks in such a slip-shod way when he has such a wonderful voice. She tells the girl to praise as well as criticise, but there is no constructive advice on how to improve poor speech.

Some of the answers are silly. A reader writes:

> DEAR SALLY,
>
> I'm going away for a winter holiday with my boy friend and his family and I am a bit worried as they are all a very sporty lot which is exactly the opposite to me. I have given my boy friend a couple of hints, but he just laughs and says I'm only lazy. I'm not lazy at all, as I have lots of energy for dancing. It's just that I hate cold weather and can't get excited at the idea of skating or ski-ing. What should I do?
>
> DEBRA (Nottingham)

The *Trend* fashion expert answered this letter:

> Why not buy some of the super looking clothes around now, and stand by looking glamorous and fragile—then he'll be happy just to have you by his side. You COULD enjoy yourself you know, without taking part in the actual sports.

This is another stupid answer to a valid question. The following reader writes on a very serious problem, and it is obvious that this girl is confused and needs guidance. The shocking thing is that she is not given it. She writes:

> DEAR SALLY,
>
> It seems to me that these days all boys only want one thing. I am sure I don't need to tell you what it is. Personally, although I am not a prude, I would never give in to a boy before marriage, and I don't particularly like letting one make love to me when I have only been out on a date with him a couple of times.
>
> The other night a boy told me I was frigid, and it's been worrying me ever since. I know I am certainly different to most of my girl friends who laugh at me, and say I'm old-fashioned. In fact, one even said I would never get married if I went on acting like this.
>
> SHARON (Harpenden)

The *Trend* psychologist replies:

> Many girls certainly behave differently these days, than two or
> even ten years ago, but the important thing is to act in a way which
> you think is right. If you have no inclination to kiss a boy until you
> are fond of him, then don't kiss him. I wouldn't say you are frigid
> just because you have got different standards, and I would take no
> notice of what your girl friends say. One day, you will meet a boy
> who will respect you for what you are, so don't try to be any different.

Sharon is asking for advice on a serious problem. She says she does
not particularly like letting a boy "make love" to her, and the
psychologist answers that she should not "kiss" a boy unless she has
the inclination. He has deliberately evaded a sincere question, and
has been quite irresponsible about it. Sharon has not been given the
answer which her very honest letter deserved. The guest star in
this case was Keith Moon of The Who, who gives the most reasonable
answer:

> Many of the boys I know are more interested in dancing, clothes
> and their scooters. Perhaps Sharon is looking for trouble of this kind
> and goes halfway to meet it, but in any case she should certainly
> stick by what she believes and if a boy gets fresh, then slap him down.
> But truly, there are lots of boys around who will date a girl for a long
> time before making any move. We aren't all sex crazy you know.

Moon is described as being:

> ... flash and extrovert. He likes things to be big and expensive,
> like the drums he thrills in banging. He likes to play every scene as
> loud as possible. Although he doesn't have a car at the moment, a
> pink Chevrolet would drive him right on to Cloud Number Seven.

Most of the readers' letters to *Valentine* deal with problems of love.
One letter shows that many young people continue to read *Valentine*
long after they have left school. The letter was from an anxious wife
who was worried about her milkman. He had been invited in for a
cup of tea and was, according to the reader, "beginning to get fresh".
The reader was advised to be out when he called or to have a
neighbour in.

The letters reveal that young people are deeply anxious about
their prospects of love and marriage. Problems dealing with appearance are a symptom of this. The moral standards adhered to in the

replies are similar to those of the strip-stories, but there is often scope for a really constructive and helpful answer which is not given.

PART III. ADVERTISEMENTS

Today the future occupation of all moppets is to be skilled consumers.

(DAVID RIESMAN, The Lonely Crowd)

Advertisements in *Trend* account for 15 per cent of the magazine. In *Jackie* 10 per cent and in *Valentine* only 3 per cent. It is difficult to find out how the pop-star features and mention of records is linked with advertising, and whether the magazines derive any actual income from these or just the assurance of increased and maintained sales. There is of course, a great deal of concealed advertising. Clothes and make-up are advertised in the fashion and beauty columns. *Jackie* runs a fashion plus advertisement column which features a new teenage boutique every week. Apart from the cut-out offers of clothes, girls discussing the magazines did not mention advertisements, but this is not strange and is no indication of how much effect the advertisements have. Recently *Jackie* has been running a travel advertisement in the form of a gossip column. The teenager is a consumer of no mean proportions, and even though he may be still at school his tastes are catered for. The advertisements in the three teenage magazines do not cover a wide range, and they fit in with the current trends. Some are excellent, especially those which advise young people not to smoke. This advertisement aims at the pocket and not at the health reason for not smoking and has a strong and immediate impact. There are also advertisements for the nursing service and the Women's Army. The other advertisements are for:

> Engagement rings
> Jewellery
> Bracelets (for men)
>
> Hair shampoos, conditioners, rinses and lacquers
> Electric rollers for setting the hair
> Cosmetics and toilet requisites
>
> Shoes
> Clothes and accessories (usually linked with fashion pages)

MORE

MONEY FOR CLOTHES & FUN IF YOU DON'T SMOKE

10 Cigarettes a day cost £30 a year or more
15 Cigarettes a day cost £45 a year or more
20 Cigarettes a day cost £60 a year or more

SO WHY SMOKE CIGARETTES AND RISK YOUR HEALTH?

Anti-smoking Advertisement—Valentine, 11 March 1967

Other publications belonging to the same company which publishes the magazine including romance strip-stories published as small booklets, and paper-backed "romances"

Musical instruments, notably guitars
Fan clubs and musical shops which sell clippings of pop stars and hard-to-get recordings
Factual notices giving details where pop stars will be performing

Patent medicines
Ointments to remove spots and pimples
Ointments to increase the size of the bust
Firms advertising "treatment" to improve the size of the bust but not indicating what this is

Mail order firms who sell a large variety of goods

The advertisements do not cover a wide range but they cater for the teenager. Apart from one advertisement for a blonde rinse, none of the advertisements could be called sophisticated. They obviously aim at type of magazine and class of reader who is uncomplicated and would not appreciate a picture of a beautiful girl sitting on a tiger-skin rug which turns out to be an advertisement for a model car. The advertisements for skin ointments, of which there are one or two in the three magazines, are the old "fear" advertisements, and are very unsophisticated.

The advertisements link up with the material in the magazines. The emphasis put on getting engaged has been shown. *Trend* publishes a full back page in colour every week, advertising engagement rings. Girls often write problem letters complaining about their appearance and saying that they are dissatisfied with their figures. The "Skinny?" advertisements offer a direct and simple remedy to every reader who worries that she is. Some of the firms advertising treatment for improved busts do not say what this treatment is. One says it "can be undertaken in the privacy of your own home". These advertisers play on the fears that the readers have of being thin and unattractive. Over a period of 8 or 9 months the advertisements have varied very little.

CHAPTER 6

Language

THE intention of the magazines is to answer a teenage demand. Their use of language is the main method of achieving this and its own particular intention is to establish common ground with readers and to exploit both the readers' want to conform and the teenage connotations of words.

It is a single, constant, esoteric type of language basically colloquial. It is concise, slangy, telegraphic, with abbreviations, pseudo-neologisms, puns, transposed jargon, short words, inverted verbless and simple sentences and short paragraphs. The esoteric language helps the teenager to believe that he belongs to an intimate club where adults and any symbols of authority are left outside. The vocabulary is limited. The following words are in current use:—

> *dead chuffed*, pleased
> *pad*, house or flat
> *the greatest*, the best
> *chicks, birds*, girls
> *pic*, picture
> *pix*, pictures
> *fave*, favourite
> *the chart*, The Top Ten Pop records
> *the disc was cut*, the record was made
> *to wax*, to make a disc or record
> *gear*, clothes
> *bug me*, annoy me
> *a loner*, a lone wolf
> *dolly*, smart, fashionable
> *aerated*, excited
> *swinging*, general word for attractive modern
> *on the fashion kick*, as regards to the latest clothes
> *vulture*, a boy who is not to be trusted

dishy, interesting or handsome
cool, (i) with-it,
     (ii) sophisticated

Girls talk about boys and say that they are "tuned in to each other's stations" The word "way-out" is extremely popular especially when used to describe clothes and habits of pop stars. It seems to mean *avant-garde*. In the strip-stories rigidity of class structure is emphasised when girls talk of boys having "posh" accents or taking them to "posh" restaurants.

The tone throughout the magazines is strongly confidential. The reader is addressed as "you" in every type of article. The magazines adopt the role of the informed adviser but pretend equal terms. We may look at how the language operates in the various features.

The pop columns show the conversational tone: "I hope I'm not being unkind when I describe the Soul Sisters as Big Bundles of Talent. They're lovely" (*Trend*).

References to the pop scene invade every article. There is an unexplained natural reference to it as if it were the whole world. In *Trend* a free knitting pattern for a not so with-it sweater is advertised as modelled by the girl "who turned down Scott Engel":

> This is Minnie—otherwise known as Irene Dunford, the girl who turned down Scott Engel. We think she refused his proposal of marriage over an intimate dinner-date, so it seems unlikely that she would have been wearing a woolly jumper like this one.
>
> However we're romantics at heart, and we fondly imagine that this sort of outfit may have helped towards capturing the heart of a Walker.

Trend makes snuff-taking appear interesting:

> Bowling through London's Haymarket with Jonas Scott, lead guitarist in his group, The Crusaders, Neil Christian said he had to stop at the famous Regency tobacconist Fribourg & Treyer to pick up an ounce of snuff.
>
> An added surprise was finding the lovely Patsy Snell, leading dancer at Murray's Carbaret Club, and Heather Tracey, soubrette at the Showboat in the Strand, who were snuff-buying too.
>
> Red-headed Patsy was buying an ounce of Macouba, which is scented with Bulgarian attar of roses and is 10s. an ounce. Blonde Heather chose Morlaix, which is a shilling more and has a fantastic aroma that can't be described. Jonas preferred one devised by James Robertson Justice. It's called Asthoroth, costs 11s. and is

made of Latakia tobacco blended with jasmine. Appropriately, Neil settled for the 9s. Princes, which was Beau Brummell's favourite—and Neil certainly looked the part, wearing a black velvet jacket braided at the edges. Other neo-Regency bucks, please note.

The above is quoted at some length because it is an example of a life quite outside the life of the provincial or suburban teenager, but because the language has the teenage stamp it is made to appear relevant. Firstly, it uses teenage slang—"bowling", "pick-up", "fantastic". Secondly, it brings in well-known, enviable names: "An added surprise was finding the lovely Patsy Snell . . ." which gives, thirdly, an impression of a scene and of an exciting unexpected event. There is also a hint of expectation suggesting that this can very well occur among "swingers".

Fourthly, "blonde", "the lovely", these descriptions of the girls make them enviably attractive. Their jobs and clubs are glibly referred to as if obviously known.

Fifthly, a tone of friendliness and gaiety gives a feeling that the stars have easy ability to handle the meeting, and there is an underlying idea that such habits show what a worthwhile person you are (the various choices of snuff also suggest this), a fashion hint, a last-line exhortation to imitate, name-dropping, technical terms and a mood of aimless gaiety.

The quotations from the pop stars are often ungrammatical. Keith Moon of the Who says: "I reckon white clothes terrifically".

The news items do not aim at factual accuracy. The facts are filtered through the reporter's opinion, and his "I think" and "I" are most important. There is a controversial element:

> Although Juke Box Jury makes people foam at the mouth, that isn't a bad thing, because it means they switch on to see what new foolishness is being perpetrated.

The style of writing makes no attempt to disguise the attitude that it can almost make up the minds of the readers: ". . . since then Rita Pavone managed to do so well with such a dire record . . . (*Trend*)".

The following fashion item in *Trend* addresses the girl-reader directly:

> From Paris so many silly trends come and after the fuss dies down, who wears the gear anyway? But here's something gimmicky that looks smart too. You wear a watch on one of your shoes, and to show

you are really showy you carry the outsize handbag with outsize key and keyhole.

The tone of the articles presume the girls want to be and are fashion-conscious. It sets up confidence and a feeling of closeness: it flatters. It is written as if every reader were an ideally pretty, lively, fashion-conscious "dolly", and if the reader ever doubts it she is at once assured that she could be. What is presented matters less than the way in which it is presented. Anything can be regarded as relevant to teenage life as long as it is introduced in a teenage manner—with teenage stamp.

Readers are not allowed to find interest in the articles for themselves. They are *told* they will enjoy an article. An artificial excitement is built up: "Get ready, all you fans of UNCLE—here comes a real bonanza of all the best of the series rolled into one" (*Trend*).

The reader feels foolish should it not be a "bonanza" for her. The same piece in *Trend* ends: "But then, they'd make up for pretty well anything, wouldn't they?"

Just as they strive to give opinions, which may be adopted, the magazines tell readers what they like.

Some articles describe the reader's likely position and, in romantic terms, suggest magical overnight success. *Trend* says:

> How many girls pounding away at their typewriters every day dream of becoming singing stars overnight? Thousands. Well it actually happened to one.
> She's Maxine Brown, a beautiful. . . .
> To her surprise, one morning she found herself a recording star with the single " It's All in My Mind"—a smash-hit in the American charts.

Articles give the impression, in giving advice, that the reader is a busy, popular and sophisticated girl, leading a full and varied life. *Trend* suggests various hair-styles:

> This style is perfect for formal evening dates.
> Marvellous if you have to dash out in a hurry. . . .
> This style is cool and tidy for town. . . .

This article suggests that any girl can look as pretty—there are stressed undertones of femininity:

> This style is very versatile—it can be worn sleekly behind the ears, in a neat page-boy, or fluffed up for a soft, casual effect. And it is

just long enough to be pinned up with a switch or false-piece for extra height.

Boys' reactions are often stressed:

> The hair is worn loose and casual, and is arranged in little-girl ringlets, caught back from the face at one side with a marguerite. A favourite with the boys. [*Trend.*]

Horoscopes make predictions in completely "teenage" terms as if those in the national press which predict such different things for adults were entirely mistaken. There is much use of nick-names, Christian names, the apostrophe and exclamation marks. The style is brief to the point of being telegraphic. There are some simple puns and quotes from songs which contribute to the esoteric "lingo".

The stock figures and situations of the strip-stories have already been studied. Basically, the language used aims to evoke these features economically. This is done by using the ready-made association or "images" of words—those with preconceived connotations for readers, so personal that perhaps the words have induced in a reader's mind an individual story, possibly a recollected personal event different from the printed one. So simple and hackneyed are the stories that it might be accurate to say that the pictures alone are all that is necessary. At times the comments are so banal as to be superfluous.

The words "love" and "dreams" appear more often than any other words. "Love" and "true love" are debased to the point where they are meaningless. It is difficult to decide whether the English is ungrammatical because the words are printed in capital letters and with very little punctuation.

The restriction of the language tends to confine thought. The heroines speak incessantly of "meeting the man of my dreams", or of "falling in love for keeps." A girl says: "Now, let's see what new talent there is in the coffee-bar today", and a few pictures later she is "really in love".

The banality of the language matches up with that of the plots. The strip-stories end either with a kiss and promise of true love or with a weeping girl, and the vocabulary is seldom varied. The weeping girl says:

> Now my tears were all too late. I knew what it was like to lose in love—and there was nothing I could do about it.

The happy girl says:

> At last my day had ended, and my life had begun. I don't know if that was a dream, darling, and this is real, but whatever it is I don't want it ever to end.

This repetitive language tends to lose all meaning and each story appears more thin and superficial than the last. Just as there is no overt sex or violence in the stories, so there is no violence in the language, but it is not just cliché-ridden; it is composed of almost nothing else but clichés.

The comments are generalised and only the pictures depict variation of situation. The essential theme of the story, the heroine's romantic confusion, is in the same words whether she is a secretary whose parents oppose her engagement or a school-teacher who marries the caretaker. The range of moods conveyed is limited to love, hate, resentment, sarcastic comment, indignation and confidence. The confidence is of a "belonging" kind—reader, I'm telling you what it feels like to be loved, to be scorned.

Excitement or intensity is conveyed by suspension marks rather than speech rhythm. There is a limited vocabulary for abuse and quarrelling. The comments of the characters are no more than an indication of a stage in the story. They do not develop states of mind; there is just basic narrative fact. Irony is always crudely obvious.

What would be a character's powerful joy, felt in his individual manner, at discovering his beloved's love for him is distilled: "Then . . . there *is* a chance for me."

A very simple psychology is used. Just one feeling motivates action: "The wedding's off. No girl keeps me waiting." The theme of the story will be a girl's conversion from one single feeling to another by a certain circumstance. A variant of the circumstances makes a new story.

The simple characterisation leads to caricature: "I've never been so insulted in my life. You keep me waiting all this time. . ."

It utilises one factor to indicate an occupation, a group, a mood, and personal association completes it.

The first person narrative is generally used; this indicates the nature of the language and its standpoint. When necessary the heroines acquire immense factual brevity and economy to tell their stories.

The themes of the strip-stories are in terms of unjustified extremes and crude dualities as between like and dislike: "My world has been shattered." "I was never surer of anything in my life."

The written stories differ mainly in elaboration. The same avoidance of complexity is concealed under longer descriptions to supplement lack of illustration, and it uses repetition, more informative dialogue and digressions. What complicates criticism of the written love stories is that, unlike other commercial fiction, the writer is not sincere, mainly because he is writing down to the reader. Another complicating factor is that the stories obey outside considerations.

Occasionally a story has a more effective theme. Such a theme was a couple's ignorance of their love for one another, their inarticulateness and assumptions that the other did not care. At a railway station, when the man was leaving to live away, there were some original expressions of "mute" love. Again, the first person gives them a uniformity; not only is the theme eternally the negotiations of obstacles to love, but from the same standpoints of prejudice and self-pity is richly introspective:

> I wished I could be sensible, cool and unflurried. I wished I knew what to say next. I wished I was in a space ship heading for the moon.

There is no striking metaphorical usage. Any attempt fails.

Let us examine one story, taken from *Trend*, the most sophisticated magazine from the linguistic standpoint.

Peter Roberts realises after several months that he loves Doreen, a girl whose persistent attention he has shunned. At first she is not as attractive as Jenny Thompson, the girl he was in love with, who scorns him as he scorns Doreen, but he thinks this unfair. When Jenny refuses point-blank to dance with him at a party he realises that he has missed Doreen's irksome letters, telephone calls and encounters.

The background of the story is vague; the encounters with the two girls occur mainly in an unnamed discotheque. Nothing in speech or character distinguishes Peter, and Jenny Thompson is just a name. Peter's age is not given though the illustration shows a man well over 20. The style of the story is almost one of contrived excitement as if it might be a thriller as when Peter first tries to avoid Doreen:

"Quick in front of me," said Peter Roberts to his friend.
"What on earth are you on about?"
"Quick, don't ask questions—shield me!"

The dialogue is more in keeping with a spy story or film.

Peter is hard and unyielding, though competent in dealing with girls. There is some compassion—the "heart of gold" theme:

> She stood there in her little canary-yellow dollyrocker dress and Peter couldn't help feeling a wave of pity tumble over him drowning his hardness.

He knows what he wants and does what he wants which is an essential ingredient of the dynamic, attractive boy friend and appears to be a basic of teenage protest and morality. He is busy—he uses this adult excuse, and gives as a reason for eluding Doreen that he has to keep appointments although his job is not given. His life is full of activity which is not really described. His speech makes him seem old and other descriptions of him give the impression of a mature, independent man. He lives with a managing mother. He talks in an unrealistic, clipped, tight-lipped way like a gangster or a Robert Mitchum character: "The least I can do is offer the poor kid a drink", his conscience said.

This is said of a girl perhaps 2 years younger than himself. His image is of a boy, self-possessed, protective, aware of the dominant, active male role. Here is another instance of hard, but kindly male coolness:

> "Like a dance, love?" he said, growing tired of standing about— and he guided her towards the crowded Saturday night floor. She snuggled up to him like a little girl on a birthday treat.

The girl submits to him, but, throughout, he is unconcerned and unflattered by Doreen's affection. He behaves like an experienced man with many women in his life. He "hails a cab" and sets her down outside her home. He "pretends not to hear" a remark of hers in the taxi. In keeping with *Trend*'s appeal to the older girl, Peter is drawn as quite a man of the world:

> He called in at a pub for a quiet drink before he went home that night. It was about seven thirty when he turned the key in the front door.

His mother greeted him on arrival. She is more like a house-keeper than a mother. His character never develops throughout the story. He is always the mature "with-it" boy who does not waste words: "You're just funny," he said, pulling a face, "but I've fallen in love with you, see."

The language creates a world in which the young girl reader can place herself. Sentences and paragraphs are short. There is simple alternation of narrative and digression. After the event comes the moral. The speech is heavily colloquial—"down to earth with a bump". It uses American expressions but is not overloaded with them. It uses words with strong teenage associations—"party" and "discotheque".

The intended effect is based on the disconnected personal pre-conceptions of the immature reader. The language suits the simple psychology of one feeling and one event. The clichés are thickly clustered—"emotion rising", for instance. Cheap rhetoric is inter-woven with the clichés:

> Doreen had disappeared for good. He didn't catch a glimpse of her, or hear a word from her—no letters, no phone calls, no turning up from the middle of nowhere to make him mad. But what was this—was he missing her? Did he pick up the phone sometimes and hope that it might be her? Impossible! He told himself, "Not that silly little scrap of a girl—not her, I wouldn't look at her sort twice."

The language helps to present an indistinct, glamorous world with which the reader can easily identify herself because nothing is concrete. There is a stock position and manipulation inside set forms and stock conversation remarks of dull and worn-out character: "pull the other leg" or "not bloomin' likely". "I was still mixed up. All I knew was I couldn't spend another night in Denise's future home."

Narrative pace is evidently insisted upon by editors. The events of a story are the objective. The language throughout the magazine is expressive for the young reader. It has no hesitancy but a directness which might be described as quick-to-paint language. In the stories, for instance, it portrays a world of simple dualities—boy *v.* girl; like *v.* dislike; homely *v.* sophistication; free *v.* tied down; boy-next-door *v.* boy with an exciting way-out job. Sophistication and glamour are overworked words, used so often that they become meaningless:

This intolerable situation continued while all the time his heart was bleeding away for someone else whose glamour and sophistication had completely thrown him.

The language sets out to make a definite impression through words of creating people and situations which are glamorous to the readers; which are half-realised already in the dreams of the readers, and to which they do and are *encouraged* to aspire.

CHAPTER 7

Analysis of questionnaires

> There is also in our view a duty on those who are charged
> with the responsibility of education to see that teenagers who
> are at the most insecure and suggestible stage of their lives, are
> not suddenly exposed to the full force of the "mass-media"
> without some counterbalancing assistance.
>
> (Crowther Report)

PART I. ANALYSIS OF COMICS AND MAGAZINES

Over 1200 questionnaires* were distributed to 4 schools within a
radius of 8 miles and were answered in February 1966. Originally
the questionnaires were to be answered by every child in a secondary
modern and every child in a comprehensive school. When the
questionnaires were returned, it was found that a number of children
had apparently been absent from school at the time, and, also, that
the numbers of children over 17 years of age answering the questionnaires in the comprehensive school was small (there was none in the
secondary modern school). In order to complete the sample the
questionnaires were answered by girls over 17 in a girls' grammar
school and boys over 17 in a boys' grammar school. The total
number of questionnaires answered was 1223 and the breakdown of
age and sex was as shown in the table on facing page.

The sample is not representative of the age group between 15 and
17 plus because it does not include any young people who are working
and receiving part-time or no further education whatsoever. The first
three groups took in the entire secondary modern school and comprehensive school who co-operated (apart from the absentees). The
secondary modern school is situated in a residential working/lower
middle-class suburb which was a small village before the war, but

---

* One of the actual questionnaires is shown in Appendix II.

			No. in sample
Group I	Boys	11–13	198
	Girls	11–13	205
Group II	Boys	13–15	249
	Girls	13–15	203
Group III	Boys	15–17	109
	Girls	15–17	117
Group IV	Boys	17 plus	76
	Girls	17 plus	66
Total no. in sample			1223

has grown with the expansion of London Airport and factories within travelling distance. The comprehensive school is in a prosperous working class area set in a sprawling outer suburb. The district has developed since the war owing to development of large factories in the area, and is typical of the unplanned expansion of Middlesex.

The girls' grammar school is in a middle-class suburb, but the pupils would not be purely local as in the case of the two former schools. The boys' grammar school is in a similar type of area, but is denominational, consequently the boys would be drawn from a bigger radius than is normal with non-denominational grammar schools.

Apart from a very small number of questionnaires which had to be marked as "spoiled", the answers appeared to be valid. The overall impression given was that the boys were more uninhibited than the girls, especially when they commented on reading sex magazines.

Table 1 is a breakdown of most of the questions asked. Some of the questions and answers were not included as they did not appear to be particularly valuable. A certain degree of error must be allowed. For instance, children were asked what other comics or magazines they read after asking if they read *Valentine*, *Jackie* or *Trend*. They were then asked at what age they started reading them. Some of the older children gave the age at which they started reading

TABLE I. READING, LISTENING, VIEWING HABITS TAKEN FROM INFORMATION ON QUESTIONNAIRES

(Figures express percentage[a])

Sex and age group	Read Valentine	Read Jackie	Read Trend	Read other light comics or magazines	Read other light comics plus serious hobbies magazines	Read hobbies/serious magazines only	Do not read comics/magazines at all	Prefer strip-stories	Prefer printed stories	Read newspapers	Read books	Buy pop records	Listen to pop programmes on radio	Watch pop programmes on TV
Boys I 11–13	2·5	2·0	4·5	70·3	22·7	2·0	5·0	68·7	21·7	84·9	52·0	45·0	78·8	77·8
Girls I 11–13	37·0	52·1	36·1	91·8	2·9	0·5	1·8	63·4	28·8	85·9	71·2	54·2	87·3	92·1
Boys II 13–15	3·6	2·0	2·8	40·1	36·2	17·3	6·4	49·9	40·1	93·2	65·1	52·6	82·0	80·0
Girls II 13–15	43·3	50·8	51·2	73·9	15·8	3·9	6·4	59·1	27·6	92·1	68·0	61·6	97·5	97·0
Boys III 15–17	4·6	0·9	3·7	15·6	30·3	42·2	11·9	28·4	54·2	98·2	45·8	65·1	92·7	85·4
Girls III 15–17	29·0	38·5	39·3	74·4	12·8	3·4	9·4	35·9	53·8	93·2	44·5	60·7	94·0	87·2
Boys IV 17 plus	4·0	4·0	4·0	7·9	15·8	59·3	17·0	2·6	64·5	96·1	52·6	35·6	77·7	54·0
Girls IV 17 plus	3·0	4·5	4·5	43·9	37·9	15·2	3·0	1·5	83·3	95·5	71·2	45·5	68·2	63·7

[a] Numbers given are percentages of the individual group samples. Except in the case of reading comics they do not add up to 100 because figures for "No" and "No answer" are omitted from this table.

publications for their age group, while others gave the age at which they started to read their first comics. It was obvious that in answering the questions "If you are reading a book at the moment, would you please give its name and the name of the author if you know it" and "Do you read any other magazines or books?", many children wrote the name of the book which they were reading as a set book or the name of a book which was part of the form library. Nevertheless, when they gave the name of the book and said they read other books, their answers were recorded as "Yes". Many children call comics and magazines "books", as do newsagents, and this must invalidate some answers.

The comics and magazines were divided, as carefully as possible, into three groups. One group was called for the benefit of the tables "light" and the other "serious/hobbies". The third small group, which was unclassifiable, was called "Miscellaneous", but this group did not enter the first broad breakdown of the questionnaires. "Light" takes in anything from sadistic American magazines to English magazines of a seemingly harmless nature. "Serious/hobbies" means that the comic or magazine had some serious content or dealt with a specific hobby. "Some serious content" ranged from the satire in *Punch* to the *Grange-Park Baptist Newsletter*.

The study so far has dealt with teenage magazines which girls read, but the questionnaires were answered by boys as well as girls. The greatest number of children came from mixed schools and the results of the questionnaires indicated such different patterns of reading habits for boys and girls that it was felt the information should not be wasted. Naturally it would be dangerous to assume that the analysis of the questionnaires is representative of groups of children all over the country, but the pattern is consistent in each group and must have significance.

It was to be expected that very few boys would read *Trend, Jackie* or *Valentine*, but a small percentage do read them, and this is repeated in the detailed analysis of comics and magazines mentioned by the sample. Evidently boys read teenage magazines which may be bought by their sisters just as girls read boys' magazines. The preference for strip-stories grew less as the age group became higher. A consistently high proportion of all groups read newspapers, and it must be remembered that in this table only one mark is recorded whether the child answers that he reads one other magazine or one other newspaper, and the same one mark is recorded if he lists several other magazines or newspapers. The detailed breakdown of comics/

magazines, newspapers and radio and television programmes is given in Table 1.

The question on reading books was not satisfactory for the reasons already given, but it was evident that girls read more novels than boys, and on the whole more boys read for factual information than do girls.

Boys and girls between 15 and 17 bought more records than any other group—65·1 per cent and 60·7 per cent respectively. Of these, 5·5 per cent of the boys and 5·0 per cent of the girls said they bought a new record every week. The lowest figure for buying pop records is 35·6 per cent for the 17-plus boys, but several of these boys said that they taped music instead of buying records.

Both sexes and all groups have high figures for listening to pop programmes on the radio and watching them on television. The girls, apart from the 17-plus girls, listen and watch more than the boys. The figures are high but the detailed breakdown will show that the range of programmes is very small.

It is not surprising to find that grammar school children staying on at school after 17 read a greater number of serious and specialist magazines than children who expect to leave school at 15 or 16. What is surprising is the great difference between the reading habits of boys and girls in every group. This will be analysed in more detail in discussing Table 2 on the actual comics and magazines mentioned, but even from Table 1 it will be seen that boys read a higher percentage of serious, hobbies or specialist magazines than do girls.

A greater number of girls than boys wanted more pictures and features of pop stars. This links up with the figures for listening and viewing pop-star programmes. A great number of boys complained about what they called "sloppy love stories", but quite a high proportion asked for more nude photographs in magazines. Both boys and girls complained about the space given to advertisement in their comics or magazines.

Table 2 gives a more detailed breakdown of the comics and magazines mentioned. It was obvious from the number of periodicals mentioned by each child that these are passed around, read in other people's homes, and, in the case of the 17-plus grammar school boys in particular, read in the school library.

In the first age group the girls named fewer comics or magazines than the boys, but they read more of those which were named. In other words, they read more of a smaller range, and their reading

TABLE 2. NUMBER OF COMICS AND MAGAZINES MENTIONED, NUMBER OF
TIMES EACH INDIVIDUAL NAME OF PERIODICAL MENTIONED AND DIVISION
INTO "SERIOUS" AND "LIGHT" TYPE OF PERIODICAL

Sex and age group	No. in sample	No. of individual comics/magazines given	No. of times comics/magazines mentioned	"Light" reader-ship (per cent)	"Serious" reader-ship (per cent)	Miscel-laneous reader-ship (per cent)
Boys I 11–13	198	97	719	85·2	14·1	0·7
Girls I 11–13	205	77	1019	97·4	1·9	0·7
Boys II 13–15	249	151	878	67·7	31·5	0·8
Girls II 13–15	203	86	996	95·5	3·1	1·4
Boys III 15–17	109	117	300	47·0	52·3	0·7
Girls III 15–17	117	55	460	89·6	5·4	5·0
Boys IV 17 plus	76	71	167	29·6	66·2	4·2
Girls IV 17 plus	66	58	200	52·0	34·5	13·5

of magazines which could claim some serious content was only 1·9 per cent as compared with 14·1 per cent serious readership by the boys of the same age. In the next age group the girls increased their serious readership to 3·1 per cent but the boys' figure jumped to 31·5 per cent. The 15–17-year-old girls claimed 5·4 per cent serious readership but compared with 52·3 per cent for the boys it is still exceedingly small. It is not until we reach the 17-plus grammar school girls that the figures for serious readership are in any way evened up, with the girls having 34·5 per cent and the boys 66·2 per cent. When recording the results of the questionnaires it was remarkable how varied were the interests of the boys compared with those of the girls.

The figures give the facts, but when you see the list of the boys' serious/hobbies periodicals and compare it with the list compiled from the girls' answers, the difference is striking. The breakdown of comics and magazines for the boys and girls in Group I is given in detail in Tables 3–6. This was done for every group, and information about further periodicals read by the other groups is given in Appendix III. The figures for the first three groups show that girls appear to have a greater love of reading than do boys, but their interests are narrower. If the desire to read is there, it is an excellent thing. A recent article in *The Guardian** stated that:

> Let us take it that eventually the C-streamer has been taught to read. But let us also face that he doesn't read for pleasure and *probably never will*. [*The italics are not mine.*]

The results of the sample disproves this. Personally, I do not like to think of children as C-streamers or A-streamers or any other kind of streamers, but if the writer means that less-able children in a secondary modern or comprehensive school do not read for their own pleasure she is quite wrong. The question facing teachers and educationists is whether reading habits can be changed.

---

* *The Guardian*, 4 April 1966, Marjorie Craddock talking about the C-stream.

TABLE 3. BOYS—GROUP I: 11–13. "LIGHT"

Name of comic or magazine	No. of times mentioned	Name of comic or magazine	No. of times mentioned
Beano	70	Diana	3
Victor	62	Woman	3
Dandy	55	Bimbo	2
Valiant	38	Beatles' Monthly	2
Topper	35	Marvel comics	2
TV 21	35	Batman	2
Hornet	34	Flash	2
Hurricane & Tiger	32	Rover & Wizard	2
Beezer	27	Men Only	2
Hotspur	26	Topless	2
Lion	22	Thor	2
Wham	21	Green Lantern	2
Buster	21	Swank	2
Smash	14	Stag	2
Superman	12	Bunty	1
TV Comic	11	Pop (Mirror)	1
Boyfriend	9	Week-End	1
War comics (4)		Popeye	1
Commando, Ace, Fleetway		Playboy	1
Picture Library, Armada	8	Mermaid	1
DC comics	6	Monster magazines	1
Sparky	6	Spiderman	1
Valentine	5	Woman's Mirror	1
Lady Penelope	5	Huckleberry Hound & Yogi-	
Parade	5	Bear	1
Classics comics	4	Princess	1
Jackie	4	Champion	1
Reveille	3	Tit Bits	1
		Total: 56 comics named	613 mentions

TABLE 4. BOYS—GROUP I: 11–13. SERIOUS/HOBBIES

Name of comic or magazine	No. of times mentioned
Boy's Own & Eagle	29
Ranger	15
Look & Learn	8
Football Monthly 4 ⎱ Soccer Star 3 ⎰	7
Autocar 2, Motorcade 1, Motor 1, Miniature Autoworld 1, The Motorbike 1, Motorcycle Mechanics 1	7
Aircraft Recognition 1, Air Pictorial 3. Aero Modeller 1	5
Knowledge	3
Angling Times 1, Anglers' World 1, Fisherman's Weekly 1	3
Reader's Digest	3
BB Steadfast	3
Railway Modeller 1, Railway Magazine 1	2
Stamp Collector's Weekly 1, Stanley Gibbons Stamp Monthly 1	2
Exchange and Mart	2
Treasure	1
Homemaker	1
Hobbies Weekly	1
Life	1
Time	1
Round the World	1
The Scout	1
EML News	1
Punch	1
Dragster & Hot Rod	1
Amateur Gardening	1
Boxing Weekly	1
Total: 37 comics named	101 mentions

MISCELLANEOUS
(Not classified)

Radio Times	1
TV Times	2
Private Eye 1, Mad 1	2
Total: 4 magazines named	5 mentions

TABLE 5.   GIRLS—GROUP I: 11–13.   "LIGHT"

Name of comic or magazine	No. of times mentioned	Name of comic or magazine	No. of times mentioned
Jackie	107	Wham	3
Bunty	87	Melody Maker	3
Judy	83	Disc Weekly	3
Valentine	77	My Weekly	3
Diana	77	True Story	3
Trend	74	Tit Bits	3
Lady Penelope	61	Reveille	3
June & Schoolfriend	60	Hornet	2
Beano	46	Hotspur	2
Dandy	43	Popeye	2
Princess	34	Record Mail	2
Woman's Own	22	Family Circle	2
Woman	21	Record Mirror	2
Topper	16	Poppet	2
Petticoat	15	Honey	2
Fabulous	14	Valiant	2
Woman's Realm	13	Huckleberry Hound &	
Beezer	12	Yogi-Bear	2
Mirabelle	11	Superman	1
Woman's Mirror	11	Pop (Mirror)	1
Beatles' Monthly	8	Rover & Wizard	1
Week-End	6	Woman & Home	1
Rave	6	Woman's Weekly	1
Lion	5	Sister Maggie	1
TV 21	5	Flair	1
Sparky	4	Music Parade	1
TV Comic	4	Bride	1
Buster	4	Showtime	1
Romeo	4	Today	1
Hurricane & Tiger	3	Photoplay	1
Smash	3	DC comics	1
Victor	3		
		Total: 62 comics named	993 mentions

TABLE 6. GIRLS—GROUP I: 11–13. SERIOUS/HOBBIES

Name of comic or magazine	No. of times mentioned
Look & Learn	5
Pony 3, *Riding* 2	5
The Guide	2
Punch	1
Knowledge	1
Fur & Feather	1
Mainly about Animals	1
Nursing Mirror	1
Reader's Digest	1
Boy's Own & Eagle	1
Total: 11 comics named	19 mentions
MISCELLANEOUS (Not classified)	
Radio Times	1
TV Times	3
Vogue	1
She	2
Total: 4 magazines named	7 mentions

Table 7 showing the most popular comics and magazines in the light and serious/hobbies classifications, was compiled from the questionnaires. The detailed list of the girls' Serious/Hobbies magazines (Table 6) illustrates that a second place in the "Most popular serious/hobbies magazines" column is not applicable. The figure would have been 2/1019 giving 0·2 per cent for *The Guide*. The same sort of situation arises in the Group II Girls and Group IV Boys.

The decision to make a detailed study of *Trend, Jackie* and *Valentine* was taken long before the questionnaires were answered. The sample figures show that they are the three most popular magazines in the

TABLE 7. MOST POPULAR MAGAZINES
(Figures represent percentages)

Sex and age group	Most popular light comics or magazines			Most popular serious/hobbies magazines		
Boys I 11–13	Beano 9·8	Victor 8·6	Dandy 7·7	Boy's Own & Eagle 4·0	Ranger 2·1	Look & Learn 1·1
Girls I 11–13	Jackie 10·5	Bunty 8·5	June & Schoolfriend 8·2	Pony and Riding Group[a] 0·5	Look & Learn —	—
Boys II 13–15	Victor 7·3	Beano 4·9	Dandy 3·8	Car and Motorcycle Group[b] 4·4	Boy's Own & Eagle 4·1	Sports Group[d] 3·5
Girls II 13–15	Trend 10·4	Jackie 10·3	Valentine 8·8	Pony and Riding Group[a] 1·5	Life 0·3	—
Boys III 15–17	Record Mirror and Victor 2·7		Beano, Playboy, Valiant, Week-end 2·3	Car and Motorcycle Group[b] 13·7	Aeroplane Group[c] 10·7	Model Eng. Group[e] 4·3
Girls III 15–17	Trend 10·0	Jackie 9·8	Woman* 8·5	Reader's Digest 1·5	Pitman's Office Training 1·1	Pony and Riding Group[a] 0·9
Boys IV 17 plus	—	—	—	Punch 15·0	Paris Match 10·2	Car and Motorcycle Group[b] 7·8
Girls IV 17 plus	Woman 14·0	Woman's Own 9·0	Honey 7·5	New Scientist 6·5	New Society 4·5	Punch 2·5

(Table notes—see following page)

13–15 age group, where they account for 29·5 per cent of the total magazines readership, and have a high rating in the 11–13 and 15–17 age groups, which points to the validity of the questionnaires. The most significant point which is brought out from the analysis of the questionnaires is that boys appear to have far more interest in hobbies and sports than do girls. Judging from the reading habits, the girls appear to read juvenile comics and teenage magazines from the age of 11. They pass on to teenage magazines and pop music magazines in the middle groups, and reach *Woman* and *Woman's Own* in the last age group. After the first age group the boys' reading shows a variety of interests. I am not giving a value judgement as to whether it is better to be interested in fashion than in repairing motor-bikes. The striking fact which emerges from the analysis is that apart from the 17-plus grammar school girls, the girls' figures show that their interests appear to be concentrated on romance, pop and clothes.

The fashion in teenage magazines has changed since the early fifties. The 13–15 girls of Group II name the following magazines which are the old-type romance periodical:

> *True Romance* mentioned 5 times
> *Love Stories* mentioned 3 times
> *Red Letter* mentioned 2 times
> *True Stories, True Confessions, Heartbeat*
> mentioned once each

---

* *Valentine* in fourth place—7·4 per cent.

a Pony and Riding Group includes: *Pony, Riding,* and *Horse & Hound.*

b Car and Motor-cycle Group includes: *Autocar, Motor, Popular Motoring, Model Car Science, Model Cars, Motor Mechanics, Motorsport, Motor Cycling, Scooter, Scooter Mechanics, Motorbike, Motorcycle Mechanics, Scooter Monthly, Motorcycle News, Track & Traffic, Speedway, Motor Cycling News, Motor Racing, Old Time Vintage Cars, Miniature, Autoworld, Motorcade, Small Cab Motoring, Ford Times, Do It Yourself Car Maintenance.*

c Aeroplane Group includes: *Air Pictorial, Aeromodeller, Airfix Magazine, Flying Review, Flight, Aircraft Review, Sud Aviation, Air Cadet, Aeronautics, BOAC Aircraft Monthly, Aircraft Recognition, Aeroplane Commercial Aviation News.*

d Sports Group includes: *Football Monthly, World Sports, Rugby World, Boxing Weekly, World Star, World Soccer, Soccer Star, Charles Buchan's Monthly, Sporting Life, Cricket Monthly, Team, Athletic Monthly, Hockey Field.*

e Model Engineering Group includes: *Practical Wireless, Woodworker, Model Maker, Hi-Fi Magazine, Practical Electronics, Radio Control, The Tape Recorder, Models and Electronics.*

This represents 14 mentions out of a total of 996. Compare this with the number of times the modern magazines are mentioned by the same group:

>*Trend*   mentioned 104 times
>*Jackie*   mentioned 103 times
>*Valentine* mentioned 88 times

The most popular serious/hobbies types of magazine for the 11–13 age group was the Pony and Riding Group and *Look and Learn,* but the figure was only 0·5 per cent which meant 5 out of 1019. It is not possible to compare the serious/hobbies type of magazines for boys and girls because it would be a one-sided affair. The long lists of magazines taken from the boys' questionnaires would produce blanks from the girls. A complete list of all comics and magazines is found in Appendix III, but the following special interest types of magazine were common to boys in all age groups:

Car and Motor Cycle Group (24 magazines were named and these are listed on p. 84)

Aeroplane Group (12 magazines named, also given on p. 84)

Sports Group (13 named; listed on p. 84)

Model Engineering Group (8 named; listed on p. 84)

Amateur Photographer and *Practical Photographer*

Angling Group which included *Fishing, Fisherman's World, Angling Times, Fishing Gazette, Angler's Mail, Fisherman's Weekly* and *Trout & Salmon.*
In Group II, 28 of this group were named.

Getting Afloat, Canoeing, Model Boats, Light Craft and *Motor Boat*

Camping, The Camper, Camping Club Monthly

Railway Magazine and *Railway Modeller*

Another interest which is shared by boys of all groups but not by girls is in the sex magazines. Table 8 illustrates this.

Two mentions of the periodical *Parade* were made by girls in Group II, therefore it was not worth including columns for girls in the table, as no other sex magazine was mentioned.

Some of the sex magazines, particularly the American publications, are quite expensive. Many newsagents do not stock them, but others sell practically nothing else, including a great many back-numbers. There is an advertisement in my local paper this week

D

TABLE 8. SEX MAGAZINES

(Figures represent the number of times the magazine was
mentioned by the particular group)

	Boys I 11–13	Boys II 13–15	Boys III 15–17	Boys IV 17 plus
Caper	—	1	—	—
King	—	—	—	1
Man's World	—	1	—	—
Man-t-Man	—	1	—	—
Men Only	2	2	2	2
Mermaid	1	—	—	—
Modern Man	—	1	—	—
Parade	5	29	11	—
Penthouse	—	6	5	2
Playboy	1	8	7	3
Skirt	—	1	—	—
Stag	2	2	—	—
Swank	2	1	1	—
Topless	2	—	—	—
Weekly Strip	—	1	—	—
Total No. of mentions	15	53	26	8
Total No. of mentions of all comics/magazines	719	878	300	167

offering back-numbers of *Penthouse* at 6*s*. 6*d*. each. Although girls
do not read American sex magazines, both boys and girls read
American comics, but as will be seen from Table 9, the numbers
are low.

The figures for boys and girls for all groups fall as they get older.
For boys, this is in relation to the figures relating to "light" as
opposed to "serious/hobbies" readership. The most popular of these
American comics is *Superman*. If the sample is any indication of
readership throughout the country it is pleasing to think that the
American comics, which are a great deal more violent and sadistic
than our own, do not have a great hold on children.

Dr. Wertham condemns American comics in his book *Seduction of
the Innocent*. He believes that the *Batman* comics are psychologically
homosexual and that *Wonder Woman* is definitely anti-masculine.

TABLE 9. AMERICAN MAGAZINES

(Figures represent the number of times the comic was
mentioned by the particular group)

	Group I 11–13 Boys	Girls	Group II 13–15 Boys	Girls	Group III 15–17 Boys	Girls	Group IV 17 plus Boys	Girls
Batman: Batboy	2		4	1				
Classics magazines	4							
DC magazines	6	1	4					
Green-lantern	2		2					
Marvel magazines	2							
Monster magazines	1		1					
Sister Maggie		1						
Superman: Superboy	12	1	17	5		1		1
Thor	2							
True Crime					1			
Wonder Woman	666		1					
Total No. of mentions	31	3	29	6	1	1	—	1
Total No. of mentions of all comics/magazines	719	1019	878	996	300	460	167	200

Wonder Woman is mentioned only once in the sample—and by a boy. While I was purchasing a copy a middle-aged housewife told me that she read two or three copies of *Wonder Woman* every week, and newsagents confirm that many adults read American comics.

The girls' teenage magazines are dominated by the pop scene, but there are also magazines which are devoted exclusively to pop music and gossip about pop stars. These are read by both sexes, but Table 10 will show that they are far more popular with girls than with boys.

PART II. ANALYSIS OF NEWSPAPERS

It is not possible to isolate one form of mass media from another. The popular dailies reduce all news to entertainment and by a series of processing which has been severely criticised by educationists, they build in and reinforce attitudes in their readers. The world of the *Daily Mirror* is as different from that of *The Guardian* as is *Valentine's*

D*

TABLE 10. POP MUSIC MAGAZINES

(Figures represent the number of times the magazine was
mentioned by the particular group)

	Group I 11–13 Boys	Girls	Group II 13–15 Boys	Girls	Group III 15–17 Boys	Girls	Group IV 17 plus Boys	Girls
Beatles' Monthly	2	8	2	4	—	6	—	—
Disc	—	—	—	2	—	—	—	—
Disc Weekly	—	3	3	2	—	—	—	—
Elvis Monthly	—	—	—	3	1	1	—	1
Fabulous	—	14	6	33	1	11	2	1
Melody Maker	—	3	4	4	3	7	2	—
Music Parade	—	1	—	—	—	—	—	—
Music Weekly	—	—	—	2	—	—	—	—
Musical Echo	—	—	—	5	—	—	—	—
Pop (Mirror)	1	1	—	1	2	—	—	—
Rave	—	6	1	25	2	13	—	2
Record Mail	—	2	—	1	—	—	—	—
Record Mirror	—	—	3	9	8	5	—	1
Record Weekly	—	—	—	1	—	—	—	—
Rolling Stones Monthly	—	1	6	—	—	—	—	—
Show Time	—	1	—	—	—	—	1	—
The New Musical Express	—	—	4	15	2	3	—	—
Total No. of mentions	3	39	24	113	19	46	5	6
Total No. of mentions of all comics/magazines	719	1019	878	996	300	460	167	200

The peak for girls in Table 10 is the 13–15 group which corresponds with the peak reading of the three teenage magazines.

from *Nova*. Although this study is concerned with magazines and comics which young people read, they were also asked what newspapers they read. The analysis shows that for boys and girls 4 or 5 newspapers score heavily over all others. Newspaper reading does not reflect the choice of the child but would normally be the choice of the parents. The *Daily Telegraph* and *Sunday Telegraph* were given a boost in Tables 11 and 12 because of their high rating with the 17-plus boys and girls.

In the fifties during the era of "The Angry Young Men", John Osborne mentioned the "posh" Sunday newspapers as though they

TABLE 11. RESULTS OF NEWSPAPER READING
TAKEN FROM THE QUESTIONNAIRES

(Figures represent number of times the newspaper was mentioned)

	Group I 11–13		Group II 13–15		Group III 15–17		Group IV 17 plus		Total
	Boys	Girls	Boys	Girls	Boys	Girls	Boys	Girls	
Daily Mirror	95	118	141	122	57	62	15	5	615
Daily Express	28	15	29	24	22	15	24	11	168
Daily Telegraph	2	6	10	6	9	10	25	26	94
Daily Mail	5	9	20	11	6	5	15	18	89
Daily Sketch	8	8	13	12	13	13	1	1	69
Sunday Times[a] } The Times	—	—	13	3	10	4	18	11	59
The Sun	8	7	9	9	12	8	4	1	58
The Observer[b]	1	3	6	3	6	3	7	17	46
Local Press Group[c]	8	10	5	8	8	5	—	2	46
Evening News	10	6	5	2	3	4	10	1	41
News of the World	5	2	10	6	9	7	—	—	39
The People	3	2	7	6	2	6	1	9	36
Sunday Mirror	11	5	6	3	1	3	2	—	31
The Guardian	—	1	4	1	—	2	5	10	23
Sunday Telegraph	—	—	3	3	3	1	1	8	19
Sunday Express	2	—	3	1	—	—	1	10	17
Evening Star	1	3	4	1	2	1	2	3	17
Financial Times	—	—	2	—	—	—	1	1	4
Sunday Post	2	—	1	—	—	—	—	—	3
Daily Worker (now Morning Star)	—	—	1	—	—	—	1	1	3
Sunday Citizen	—	1	—	1	—	—	—	—	2
Total No. of mentions	189	196	292	222	163	149	133	135	

[a] It was often impossible to tell from the answers whether the reply meant *The Times* or *The Sunday Times*.

[b] As in the case of *The Observer*, the *Colour Supplement* was often mentioned and this was recorded as the name of the paper to which it belongs.

[c] Local Press Group includes: *Middlesex Chronicle*, *Richmond & Twickenham Times*, *Hayes Gazette*, *Hayes News*, *Hillingdon Mirror*, *Hillingdon News* and *Toronto Star Weekly*.

were not read by ordinary people. The quality Sundays account for a reasonably high figure in Table 11. This might have something to do with their colour supplements which were mentioned frequently in the questionnaires. The three most popular newspapers with their percentages of readership are given in Table 12.

Raymond Williams in *The Long Revolution* says that the readership in the "quality" papers continues to rise steadily, but he thinks it is

TABLE 12. THREE MOST POPULAR NEWSPAPERS READ BY EACH GROUP

Sex and age group	No. of individual papers named	Total No. of mentions	Three most popular newspapers		
			I per cent	II per cent	III per cent
Boys I 11–13	15	189	Daily Mirror 50·2	Daily Express 14·8	Sunday Mirror 5·8
Girls I 11–13	15	196	Daily Mirror 60·2	Daily Express 7·7	Daily Mail 4·6
Boys II 13–15	18	292	Daily Mirror 48·2	Daily Express 9·9	Daily Mail 6·9
Girls II 13–15	17	222	Daily Mirror 55·0	Daily Express 10·8	Sketch 5·4
Boys III 15–17	15	163	Daily Mirror 35·0	Daily Express 13·5	Sketch 8·0
Girls III 15–17	15	149	Daily Mirror 41·6	Daily Express 10·1	Sketch 8·7
Boys IV 17 plus	18	133	Daily Telegraph 18·8	Daily Express 18·1	Daily Mail Daily Mirror 11·3[a]
Girls IV 17 plus	17	135	Daily Telegraph 19·3	Daily Mail 13·3	Observer Colour Supplement 12·6

Average percentages of all groups who read *Daily Mirror* 41·6 per cent.
[a] *Daily Mirror* in 4th place, 3·7 per cent.

significant that there is a rise in the tabloid press and also in magazines of a similar character.

As I have pointed out, it is not quite fair to make a judgement on the newspapers that the children named, as most of them were probably chosen by their parents. On the other hand, it is obvious that if a child stays on at school after 15 he has more chance of being exposed to better types of magazines and newspapers. The figures Tables 11 and 12 emphasise the contraction in the numbers of papers available to the public. The readership of the local press group is quite encouraging, but, of course, when compared with the popular giants it is insignificant.

PART III. ANALYSIS OF RADIO AND TELEVISION PROGRAMMES

It is natural to expect that the length of a child's stay at school after the minimum school-leaving age should reflect his taste in reading and leisure activities. Even on such a small sample taken in only one area of the country, it is obvious that the child who stays on at school after 15 has more resistance to the reading of comics, non-serious magazines and the popular press. Pop music, however, is the common interest of boys and girls between the ages of 11 and 17. The children who answered the questionnaires must have had a wide range of intellectual ability and educational opportunity. Thus the appeal of pop is more than purely musical; it is an identification with a certain way of life and with the "teenager" image which the teenage listeners recognise as being conveyed through only a few programmes. Tables 13–15 do not illustrate the whole pattern of listening and viewing habits of the young people answering the questionnaires.

They were asked:

> Do you listen to pop stars on the radio? Yes/No. If you answered "Yes", what is the best programme for this?

and

> Do you watch your favourite pop stars on TV? Yes/No. If you answered "Yes", what is the best programme for this?

The percentages who gave "No" or "No answer" to this question from the different groups are shown in Table 13.

The numbers who do not listen or look at pop programmes are undoubtedly higher in the 17-plus group, but those who do so share

TABLE 13

		Radio per cent	Television per cent
Boys I	11–13	21·2	22·2
Girls I	11–13	12·7	7·9
Boys II	13–15	18·0	20·0
Girls II	13–15	2·5	3·0
Boys III	15–17	7·3	14·6
Girls III	15–17	6·0	2·8
Boys IV	17 plus	22·3	46·0
Girls IV	17 plus	31·8	36·3

the same preferences as the other groups. Many of the boys and girls in Group IV were annoyed when asked whether they read the teenage magazines, *Jackie*, *Trend* and *Valentine* which devote so much of their space to pop star gossip, and they demonstrated this annoyance by writing remarks on the questionnaires. Where they meet on common ground with the other groups is in sharing decided preferences for the same programmes. As shown in Table 14, of the 17-plus girls who do listen to pop programmes, 53·3 per cent of them follow the most popular radio programme which is, in fact, not a programme but a pirate station, Radio London.

Of those children who look and listen to pop programmes there is a frightening conformity in their choice. The same three programmes are featured in every group except the last group of girls over 17 who have a different programme for the third place. Table 15 emphasises that boys and girls of all intellectual levels meet on common ground when it comes to pop programmes on radio and television.

The reason for this lies in the history of pop programmes which, of course, is not very long. About 10 years ago there was one programme which was on the BBC television service. It was Juke Box Jury and it had no competitors. It was the only outlet for pop music. It influenced the sale of records and when it plugged a record that record was sure of success. The disc jockey was—and still is—David Jacobs. ITV produced their answer to Juke Box Jury which was

TABLE 14. RESULTS OF ANALYSIS OF POP PROGRAMMES ON RADIO AND TELEVISION

(Figures represent number of times programmes were mentioned)

	Group I 11–13 Boys	Girls	Group II 13–15 Boys	Girls	Group III 15–17 Boys	Girls	Group IV 17 plus Boys	Girls	Total
Radio London	82	88	125	150	72	87	35	19	658
Top of the Pops (BBC TV)	113	114	116	105	47	59	19	31	604
Ready Steady Go (ITV)	42	66	74	106	44	61	8	7	408
Radio Luxembourg (Commercial)	17	19	18	19	9	25	5	3	115
Pick of the Pops (BBC Light)	1	24	19	19	10	6	5	9	99
Radio Caroline[a]	13	14	19	11	3	4	—	—	64
Thank Your Lucky Stars (ITV)	11	12	9	11	1	3	1	—	48
Saturday Club (BBC Light)	4	6	6	6	1	3	1	1	28
Easybeat (BBC Light)	2	3	6	8	2	1	—	—	22
Children's Favourites (BBC Light)	7	3	—	3	1	—	—	1	15
A Whole Scene Going (BBC TV)	—	—	—	3	—	8	2	—	13
Family Favourites (BBC Light)	3	6	1	—	—	—	—	—	10
12 o'clock Spin (BBC Light)	—	2	2	1	—	—	—	—	5
Housewive's Choice (BBC Light)	1	2	—	—	—	—	—	—	3
Roundabout (BBC Light)	—	2	—	—	—	—	—	1	3
5 o'clock Club (ITV)	1	—	—	—	—	—	1	1	3
Juke Box Jury (BBC TV)	—	1	1	—	—	—	—	—	2
Arthur Haynes Show (ITV)	1	—	—	—	—	—	—	—	1
Total No. of mentions	189	196	292	222	163	149	133	135	

[a] This station was recently put out of action because of damage to the ship, and this might account for the low figures compared with Radio London (Radio Caroline and Radio London are both pirate stations).

TABLE 15. BREAKDOWN OF MOST POPULAR RADIO AND TV PROGRAMMES

	No. of stations or pro-grammes named	No. of mentions	Three most popular programmes			Total of three most popular as percentage of all pro-grammes and stations men-tioned
			I per cent	II per cent	III per cent	
Boys I 11–13	14	304	Top of the Pops 37·1	Radio London 27·0	Ready Steady Go 13·8	77·9
Girls I 11–13	17	363	Top of the Pops 31·4	Radio London 24·2	Ready Steady Go 18·2	73·8
Boys II 13–15	13	398	Radio London 31·4	Top of the Pops 29·2	Ready Steady Go 18·6	79·2
Girls II 13–15	13	443	Radio London 33·9	Ready Steady Go 23·9	Top of the Pops 23·7	81·5
Boys III 15–17	11	191	Radio London 37·7	Top of the Pops 24·6	Ready Steady Go 23·0	85·3
Girls III 15–17	11	258	Radio London 33·7	Ready Steady Go 23·6	Top of the Pops 22·9	80·2
Boys IV 17 plus	10	78	Radio London 44·9	Top of the Pops 24·4	Ready Steady Go 10·3	80·1
Girls IV 17 plus	9	73	Top of the Pops 43·5	Radio London 26·1	Pick of the Pops[a] 12·3	80·9

[a] Ready Steady Go, 4th place, 9·6 per cent.
Radio London—Pirate Station.   Pick of the Pops—BBC Light programme.
Ready Steady Go—ITV.   Top of the Pops—BBC TV 1.

Thank your Lucky Stars. As far as the teenagers were concerned it was better and more popular than Juke Box Jury because it had pop stars appearing in person in it.

As the interest in pop grew, the pop-star cult developed and the sales of records soared, radio and television directors took pop more seriously and provided other programmes. ITV launched Ready Steady Go.* They invited teenagers to take part, and all that was necessary was to queue up before the show. The teenagers appeared on the screen dancing to the music. Then the promoters thought of a brilliant idea. They chose an ordinary girl from the suburbs of London with no singing or dancing ability. She represented the ordinary teenagers watching the programme. She wasn't particularly beautiful or clever; she didn't talk down to the young girls, she was just one of them. This was the turning point of pop television programmes. It made the teenagers feel tremendously important in themselves. Juke Box Jury is still running, but as will be seen from the figures it is not popular with young people. It has not changed very much since its inception, and it is run by David Jacobs, who, according to teenage standards, is definitely old.

A Whole Scene Going, which was too new to have any influence on the questionnaires, looked as if it would be popular at the start of its single series. Teenagers I spoke to thought it would be popular. Run entirely by young people, if not by teenagers, it took teenagers seriously while not patronising them. It had a format similar to the magazines, with pop star interviews, fashion, make-up and dieting hints, though directed to a slightly older age group. However "live" performances did not reproduce the sound of records, more obscure pop stars and "purists" like jazz and blues singers were too much featured, and in the end it was too analytical of the mystique which current pop shows just exploit.

Since it began, Top of the Pops, the highest-rated television pop show, because it just straightforwardly presents the hit tunes, has developed a comprehensive pop entertainment. Now the stars sing their hits instead of miming to the records. Flashing lighting effects illuminate the invited audience of dancers in the studio; the viewers see vivid swirling patterns on their screens; films about the groups using extreme camera effects and edited to the rhythm of the music sometimes accompany the songs. A rota of senior disc jockeys preside.

* ITV have now taken off this programme.

The popularity of the pirate radio stations,* Radio London in particular, has eclipsed Radio Luxemburg because it is on all day. Teenagers can hear what they want to hear—nothing but pop records. It is informal, and the disc jockeys talk the same language as the young people. They are uninhibited and do not appear to be restricted in the same way as are BBC disc jockeys. This is partly because the comment is entirely unscripted, and the disc jockeys say exactly what they think. This is not to say they are not absolutely professional. One of them, Simon Dee, late of Radio Caroline, was interviewed recently and said that he was sent hundreds of presents. When he announced that one of the staff was ill, hundreds of little boats appeared to take him ashore. Mr. Dee, who now has a programme on the BBC Light programme, said it was like Dunkirk.

It was not unusual to read on the questionnaires: "Fabulous Radio London, wonderful Radio London, Radio London all the time."

Just as the whole pop scene does not remain static so the television and radio programmes change and top popularity does not last for ever. Ready Steady Go was a firm favourite when it first came out about 2 years ago, and now comes in third place with five of the groups.

---

* On August 14th, 1967 all but two (Caroline North and South) of the pirate radio stations were closed by order of the Marine Broadcasting (Offences) Act.

CHAPTER 8

What the school-girls say

ALL the girls interviewed had strong allegiances to particular magazines. Even pairs of friends differed in their preferences; one would prefer *Jackie* and the other *Trend*. If a girl bought only one magazine she would read others by borrowing them. The girls, between 13 and 16, were willing to talk but had to be helped to express themselves:

> "Its got more in it", or
> "Its got better stories," or
> "Its a good mixture," or
> "Its got more fashion and stuff"—

these were the main reasons for preferring one magazine rather than another. This was said of most of the magazines and although it was apparent that particular magazines were more to their taste, they found it difficult to enlarge on the factors of appeal.

It can be said without any doubt that all the girls interviewed were enthusiastic about the magazines. They read them avidly. They were a good cross-section of pupils from a secondary school, and those staying on after the statutory school-leaving age and doing more academic work were able to criticise the magazines in a discriminating way, but, nevertheless, still read them and valued them. Almost all the girls spontaneously expressed aversion to reading books connected with school work, or to reading full-length books for pleasure. These books were spoken of with derision, in fact there was down-right hostility towards them. It was sometimes confusing because "I read my Mum's books too", often meant reading Mum's *Woman* or *Family Circle*.

Girl after girl said she did not mind reading paper-backed books such as UNCLE books, horror paper-backs or Batman paper-backs.

E

The one thing which was obvious and made itself felt throughout the interviews was that *the girls wanted to read something*.

One girl read seven magazines each week: "I get them from my friends and my cousin."

Another said:

> I read them more in the holidays. I go round the estate changing them with my friends. If we bring them to school we sometimes get them confiscated.

One girl was able to read the whole range on her paper round. The girls were familiar with back numbers; they instantly recognised covers of issues even 6 months old.

Reasons for reading the magazines came in the following order:

> I like the love stories.
> I can't read enough of the stories. I buy *Valentine* because it's got more in it to read.

Second in popularity were the pop articles and pop gossip, then came the problem letters, the fashion and beauty hints and the pop-letter columns and pin-up photographs.

Their attitudes to the stories were not varied. They said they liked them with some enthusiasm, but seemed unable to form individual judgements. Talking in small groups of three or four they became more articulate. They realised that the stories depicted an idealised dream-world. They said the boys in them were attractive, but

> They are all dark or blonde, all well-built. They are not real. There are no mediums.
> The stories always work out well, but that's not like real life.

Several girls called them "unreal" and "like dreams".

One girl who declared that she had "been out with" fifteen boys said:

> The girls in the stories are too lucky. They always get a lovely boy in the end. They have a bit of upsets in the middle, but in the end it always comes all right. In real life you never get the boy you really want. . . .

Most girls enjoyed the escapism:

> The people aren't really doing the things you do in everyday life. All the girls are pretty although they do dress up a bit for parties. We never dress up like that for parties; you can go in anything.

They recognised that none of the boys in the stories was ever very poor or plain, and that only rarely did a story end in a wedding. There was no concern that they should end in marriage. The essential concern was to enjoy yourself with the boys and to have a regular boy friend. Some admired the idea of the characters, boys or girls, in the stories having flats of their own, but said these were the sort of people of whom mothers and fathers did not approve: "My friend's sister has got her own flat up London, but Mum and Dad wouldn't let me go there." The girls were aware that the stories were similar in all the magazines and that stock plots recurred. They accepted this.

"I like *their* stories best" was given time and time again as a reason for reading a certain magazine. *Valentine*, which contains most printed matter and more actual stories, was the least popular of the three magazines among the girls interviewed, but the printed stories were quoted almost as much as the strip-stories although the latter appeared to be even more of a relief from school-reading. The girls were impressed by the politeness and smartness of the boys in the stories:

> They never swear. The blokes round here never stop swearing. These others in stories take them out to nice places, keep saying nice things. Here you always go either to people's houses or pictures.

A 14-year-old said:

> Boys in the club are never like that. They all stick together and just want to show off in front of their mates.

There was some self-identification. Some girls wished that their lives would turn out the same as the girls in the stories. One 13-year-old said that the stories helped her to look forward to things; it was an impression of how dating would be. The girls found the stories compelling. They stressed this, though they realised their unreal, superficial nature. Once started, their interest was held to the end. The serials were thus a reason for continuing allegiance to a particular magazine:

> Yes, I remember that serial. My Mum used to try to get hold of it before me so that she could read it first.

The girls did not connect the love-story world with theirs. Rather they enjoyed the escapism and only mildly envied the good luck, money, good looks, cars, flats and scooters which featured in the lives of the fiction characters. One girl sought for identification and said:

> I like the stories where the girls lose their boy friends because that has happened to me. If you get a nice boy friend someone comes along and pinches him just as they do in the stories sometimes.

And she compares this with books she has been "made to read".

> The books *they* make us read are like fairy stories. You can't get into them. I can get into my *Valentine* stories right away. I can pick it up and have a read but other books are too dry; they are boring. They confiscate our magazines if we read them in the classroom. *They* want us to read old-fashioned books.

Presentation was an important reason for allegiance. The colour photographs in *Jackie* and *Trend* were popular. Almost all the girls collected the pictures of pop stars and many pinned them up at home. One of the main reasons for reading the magazines was that they provide information about and photographs of their current stars. Not one girl said she had written to the advice/problems columns but several had written to the sections which gave news and gossip of the pop world. The magazines give fuller identity to the remote stars: "They tell you who they're friends with, what they're like, what new records they are making."

One girl said the pop stars became more real as people. The girls avidly stored details of their favourites; they spoke about them as if they had met them—of Scott Walker, one of the Walker Brothers, a girl said:

> He's got a girl he wants to marry. But Eileen won't marry him for three years. She says he goes out with other girls and he says she sees other boys.

Some girls tended to read magazines which they thought featured their favourite groups and allegiances varied according to this:

> You sort of know everything about them—if they wear red pyjamas with pink spots on. They put in a lot of rubbish about them,

said one girl. Another spoke for several when she said:

> No, I don't believe everything I read about them. I know lots of it is just publicity, but I like reading about them just the same.

Most of the girls bought pop records. This was followed up by an appetite for details about the pop stars and they went to the magazines to find these details. "The stories don't matter. The magazines have to be up to date about the pop stars."

The girls want strict topicality and accuracy. One girl had written to *Valentine*: "They gave Ringo's birthday wrong and I wrote up and told them about it."

Another girl said:

> I don't know why I keep on reading about them. They make out these pop stars are all original and unusual and most of the things they say they do are just drippy. Like today in *Jackie*, Zoot Money says his hobbies are eating and reading magazines. Some of the things are too stupid to really believe.

The girls were interested in the fashion columns but were unanimous in saying: "I wouldn't buy a magazine just for the fashions. *Petticoat* is all fashions with nothing much to read."

Jackie and *Trend* were considered to be reasonably good on fashions although some girls said that the dress patterns featured were impracticable:

> They're supposed to be bargains, but when you've sent up for them and you get them they cost a lot more than dresses from the shop.

It was risky also to send away for cut-out clothes: "You don't know till you get them—they could be flops."

Yet one girl bought *Trend* because of the fashion offers:

> I wish they had more fashion and budgets and hints on how to make mod clothes. I often send away for their offers and they are good. The trouser suit offer was only 49*s* 11*d*. and it was good and worth it.

This girl was nearly 16 and quite confident and mature for her age. She wanted to be a window-dresser or caterer and was more advanced in her views on fashion than many of the younger girls who did not apply the hints offered on the fashion pages. These girls had an abstract interest in clothes. The sort of clothes which they themselves wore were not shown. The clothes on the fashion pages had, to them, the same romantic interest as the stories offered.

The problem letters were very popular. Some girls had written funny letters on their experiences to the magazines which paid for those published. If little actual notice was taken of fashion hints, then advice about problems was regarded. The idea of exposing personal facts was not basically abhorrent: "We like the letters. We sometimes laugh at them."

Most girls took them more seriously, even the same girl added: ". . . until those things happen to you."

Another girl said:

> I think the letters are real. I think of myself sometimes, especially when I've had a row with Mum and Dad about what time to come in. Its awful when you go to a party, you meet a nice boy and he wants to take you home . . . you have to say to him "My Dad is coming to fetch me".

Some girls said they would like to write seeking advice. It seemed that most of them would as soon write up as approach their parents. They recognised the problems as familiar; they took the difficulties seriously: "Sometimes when I read a letter from a girl I think I could have written that myself."

The magazines are basically a relief from school-work. They can be read at will, are shorter than books, written in a style of which the girls approve and have pictures for extra interest. They give the girls a feeling of personal identity, but they also give them a sense of belonging to a great club:

> I like them because they are for teenagers and they are about the things we like. I think school stories are drippy now and other books are dead boring.

A girl in her examination year said:

> We have to do a lot of work. At least the magazines are exciting. Its better than plain books.

Another girl said:

> You can have a quick look at the pictures first and then read them. With a book you have to sit down for a long time to read it.

An Indian girl who had been in the country for only 2 years said she loved the magazines and read them regularly; they did not have similar magazines for teenagers in India.

One girl called the educational magazines ". . . a lot of old rubbish!"

It did not occur to the girls that there was anything else to read. They sneered at educational magazines such as *Knowledge* or *Animal World*. One rather serious girl who said she would like to work with animals (a very common ambition among girls of the 13–15 age group) said she had never heard of *Animal World* or any other serious magazines dealing with animals. Very few girls were interested in reading newspapers, even the popular papers. On average they glanced at them about twice a week. It did not occur to them that there was anything else to read. A girl said she could think of no alternative to reading teenage magazines:

> There's not much else to read except the square books we get in the library. The only books I read are Man from UNCLE, *Beatle's Weekly* and paper-backs.

Paper-back novels were the only form of book fiction which most of the girls would read. Many girls could suggest no alternative form of reading except set-books and text books which were disliked. The magazines provide the only form of reading matter which has a direct relation with their own lives even if they falsified and idealised them. The magazines inform them of the trends of fashion for their age group, keep them in touch with the pop world and provide them with agreeable easy-to-read fiction. Through the magazines they feel identity with other young people: "You've got to be young and with it." "It helps you to be with it."

Other books and magazines had nothing specifically to do with the teenage girl's world. One girl was seeking to put into words how the magazines helped her to conform in dress and jargon: "It makes you alike", she said.

CHAPTER 9

Conclusions

THE teenage magazines in vogue at present have been in existence for about 10 years, but in the early sixties their formula changed from the predominant strip-stories of a romantic appeal, and now in the mid-sixties they are a mixture of strip-stories (still with a romantic appeal) and pictures and gossip about pop stars. Their esoteric quality is most pronounced to the reader who is not a teenager. They are written in special teenage language which encourages young people to become part of the pop-culture teenage group resenting interference from any other forms of authority. As mentioned in Chapter 2, when parents do appear as characters (which is seldom), they are drawn as sour, elderly people, whereas most parents of today's teenagers would be in early middle age. This situation might be a consequence of decrease in parental, church and school authority which has been taking place since the Second World War. It is interesting to contrast this attitude towards older people with the situations in stories in romantic magazines published in India. Many of these stories deal with the conflict between the heroine's desire for a love marriage and the parents' plans for an arranged marriage. In all these Indian stories, respect and a wish to please the parents is strongly stressed. Many overseas students are shocked at the freedom which young people are given today. We may decry the way in which overseas children are brought up, but as one gets older it is rather pleasant to think that in the East respect is still conceded to older people—just because they are older. If we wish to influence young people in this country today, merely being older is not enough.

From the tone of the letters published in the teenage magazines one gathers that the teenagers are drawn into a dream world of superficial romance and made to believe that they are part of the pop-music vanguard. There is a strong contradiction between the lives of the strip-story characters and those of the pop stars. Identification with the strip-story characters is simple for the reasons pointed out in Chapter 2. This identification is also possible with the majority of the pop stars who come from working-class homes, have been to secondary modern schools, and are good to "Mum and Dad". Because they have a great deal more money, the pop stars are allowed to indulge in expensive clothes, cars and ultra-modern houses. In fact, this trivia is churned out by the teenage magazines as long as the pop stars remain fashionable.

Readers' readiness to believe that they can be improved, and helped to conform through being appropriately informed reveals two tenets fundamental to the magazines' success. The first belief is that every girl possesses a personality, distinct as a commodity which she has bought. The second is in the infinite perfectibility of personality. Their personality is not generated, in this view, by response to living experience, but is equal to the sum of outer habits and looks. The whole pop scene is founded on the idea that you can improve yourself by adoption of the correct external features, that you can be altered from outside by your choice of dress, hair-style, make-up, speech and jargon. These outward factors make up what a person is:

> The way you wear your hair can change your image completely from one day to another and as most of us like to be mysteriously alluring when we're out on our dates we're forever ringing the changes. No two boys even see we girls in the same light and as I generally seem to be playing it casual one minute and sophisticated the next, it's a great advantage to be able to change my hair-style just as easily as turning on a tan.

In this way the pop scene, reinforced by the ethos of the magazines, has misinterpreted the idea which psychology produced of fluid, changeable personality. There is a theory that, with a change in certain forces which influence a person, his nature might itself be changed and the pop world has wrongly chosen alteration of external appearance as the mode of change. Thus, the immense emphasis on appearance, not natural physical appearance, but on how one looks after adornment, is explained. The motive for avid adherence to the magazines, then, is the search for a particular means of change to a better personality.

Therefore, if you collect odd objects, this expresses your personality. Hence The Small Faces stress their collection of toy, mechanical robots to display their zany individualism, and another group boasts of its gun collection. Here, what is essentially an indulgence of childish likes, in their case for guns, that groups are enabled to afford, is passed off as a commendable eccentricity expressive of their difference. Again, if, as in *Valentine*, a group member calls a cat a "moggie-cat" it conveys to the reader his whole personality through his particular zany talk.

A consequence of the attitude is the feeling that being a person, and also personal relations, are a knack, a matter of acquired method. If a body-building course will give you happiness by changing the shape of your physique, then, similarly, personality can be shaped. The magazines have an unprofessed undertaking to teach their readers.

These unspoken assumptions, half-beliefs and motivations underly the magazines. The actual coverage which has developed is, in a sense, arbitrary, but, in having its own effects, it needs to be studied. The very way in which the magazines are written is the chief method of impact (firstly, because, of course, the magazines are written), and, secondly, because at the same time as the given facts have their direct effect, the way of giving them is having deeper, indirect effects through creating the identity between magazine and reader and setting up the standards of conformity.

The girls in the strip-stories do not usually marry rich boys with pink Jaguars, but they do like to have new dresses for Saturday night dating, buy records and cosmetics and have enough money for entertainment. These magazines cater for the young worker and the girl who will soon become the young worker, and references to studying or staying on at school or college is always in the derogatory sense. The range of advertisements is small, but it relates to the values presented, and concentrates upon the teenage market.

The trend setters in the pop scene, whether in the media of magazines or radio and television programmes appear to the teenager to come from within his own group, and are not people imposed upon him by recognised forms of authority. It was important to touch on other forms of mass media apart from teenage magazines, because the pop scene has had a tremendous influence in all these different forms, and the standardisation of popular images has a powerful effect. In fact, it has a reinforcing effect. The average teenager is not aware of the fact that the businessmen and promoters behind the scenes are contriving the whole situation to make it appear that adults are not involved. The popular magazines of today are in the hands of the same small, but dominating group of publishers who have been producing cheap mass-selling periodicals for years. D. C. Thomson publish *Red Letter* and *Red Star Weekly*, the old type of romantic magazine for young girls containing printed stories. As the figures from the questionnaires show, this type of magazine has fallen out of favour, but the same company also publishes the very popular *Beano*, *Dandy*, *Bunty*, *Diana*, *Judy* and *Jackie*. This situation is analogous with that of the recording companies who have all made huge profits out of the currently popular singers and musicians. A glance through the *Financial Times* will confirm this.

A typical example of the shrewdness of the men behind the scenes is the success of *Batman* which exemplifies commercial exploitation in several areas. It began as an American adventure-horror magazine. A 4-hour omnibus film of episodes from an old *Batman* television series was then successfully shown in New York as part of the interest in "camp" (deliberately "corny" art and design) and was moved to London. It was successful and was followed by a new children's series of Batman adventures (similar to the self-parody, UNCLE) shown twice a week on television. Intentionally, acting is ham, plots far-fetched and the ridiculously exaggerated villains are shown as obsessed with some fetish. Good and evil are crudely differentiated. "Batman", the alias of a millionaire, breaks off his fight against crime to point out lessons on citizenship and proper behaviour. Again, sales of Batman music and goods boomed. The programme is part of the "zany human" trend.

It would be unfair to think that all teenagers are naïve about the commercial instinct for money-making behind the pop scene. It is difficult to decide whether there is a completely uncritical attachment to the cheap, popular magazines. What the questionnaires do reveal is that the more mature, more discriminating and, of course, older grammar school children reject most of the cheap stuff and introduce more serious and worthwhile magazines into their reading. On the other hand, the number of children who are rated as "non-academic" and who read *The Observer* and The *Sunday Times* colour supplements is surprisingly high. This leads us to ask whether a good, professional and fashionable magazine catering for a bigger variety of interests would sell among young people. The one thing that would kill it would be to write down to them.

The problem letters in the teenage magazines show that many girls are genuinely seeking advice. Today young girls may see the most candid plays on television, but the magazines have an evasive, old-fashioned flavour. A magazine catering for young people would do well to consider publishing straightforward, honest articles about sex on similar lines to those in *New Society*, which, incidentally, is popular with the grammar school girls over 17.

The romance world in the magazines is one removed from reality, where "love" upsets have no emotional harm. Certainly, the stories do not disturb; they assure, give an idea of a too simplified unrealistic life, and often lead to parental antagonisms as parents symbolise frustration of romance. They give a black-and-white romance idea of love and what to expect from life which might be dangerous if applied practically by the readers.

The difference in reading habits between the children who stayed in school after 17, and those who were under 17 is striking. For boys over 17 the three most popular "light" comics or magazines could not be given, as the list of periodicals named showed that out of the 22·7 per cent "light" magazines mentioned, there was no addiction to any particular one, and the percentage figures for the three most popular were too low to be significant.

The girls over 17 had a higher proportion of "light" reading— 43·1 per cent. This higher figure arises because of the relatively high proportion of girls reading women's magazines. Many of the women's magazines are of a far higher quality than the three teenage magazines described in this study. They have excellent fashion, cookery and other articles concerned with the home, dress and beauty. It might be argued that it is just as worthwhile for a girl to knit herself a jumper as for a boy to take his motor-bike to pieces. This is perfectly valid, but the allegiance that girls and women give to women's magazines is pernicious. It is because they are magazines *for women* that they are pernicious. The best way to keep people ignorant is to keep them ill-informed. In our machine age it is vital for women to keep up the traditional arts of being able to run a home well, be able to cook and to sit down and make her child a fancy dress. But if women are not to be second-class citizens, and looking at the figures for women's entries into the universities and the professions it is plain that women are underprivileged in this respect (unless one argues, of course, that they are more stupid), they must be able to play their part in the community and to be in a position to voice their own special needs and those of their children. The dreams of the early suffragettes have not been realised, and one has to admit that it is difficult for a woman to have any outside interests at certain periods of life, but the women's magazines have encouraged women to be home-makers and leave the decisions to men.

In 1960 a conference on "Popular Culture and Personal Responsibility" was convened by the NUT. Mrs. Dora Russell, who represented the International Committee of Mothers, spoke thus on women's magazines: ". . . I feel that nobody takes the business of women's magazines sufficiently seriously."

Mrs. Russell said that they are really men's magazines because they are a good market for advertising firms, and she went on to say:

> They do present an image of women which is the kind of women that men want to have, and unfortunately, this kind of woman is expected to remain at home and take no interest in outside affairs.

This attitude is developed early and can be related to the almost slavish addition girls have for three or four magazines with high circulation, while the boys of their own age group read a variety of magazines revealing their many hobbies and outside interests. It is now generally agreed that inequalities in educational opportunity arise from social factors and geographical location; sex should be added to these two. Girls tend to leave school earlier than boys; they receive less further education and far fewer of them reach professional standards. If our common culture is to be shared by men and women alike, we must not underestimate the pernicious influence of teenage magazines and women's magazines. The harm from this type of literature is the persistent encouragement to "dream" rather than to "do" or to participate.

The wide adherence to the magazines is another reflection of women's limited role and opportunity for careers. Feeling little incentive to study, girls, especially the "Newsom" girl, turn to them; and once they get used to "easy" reading, progress is further impeded. As well as reflecting the limited life, the magazines serve to further limit life, for they present existing life as having attractions if approached correctly; they do not encourage expanding interests. A regrettable point to note is that readers seek not only escapism but practical help which they accept wholeheartedly. The whole attachment shows a preoccupation with entertainment and fun, and with the mode of life, instead of life itself. The magazines support, confirm and perpetuate the restricted lives and ideas of the typical reader; the 15-year-old school-leaver who is engaged, perhaps by 16 or 17 and married by 20.

In a commercial society the early leaver is not just a consumer. He is a necessary expendable operative unskilled or semi-skilled. Much has been said and written about making use of the increased leisure time which technological developments will give. It is discussed at every teachers' conference and teachers are exhorted to give pupils a taste for the "full life"—a life with plentiful, rewarding recreation, including, perhaps, worthwhile reading. For if young people were helped to read in a discriminating manner this could be one means of enabling them to resist automatic enslavement to machine tending. This does not advocate return to craft or domestic industry: automation as a process of production will, I believe, look after our needs. When teachers, knowing the promise of a "full life" see young people leave school, might they not wonder how little they have really done? In the society of science and automation it is the teacher's job, perhaps, to keep people human—not just alive, but human. Most children, after 10 years at school, and having doubted its practical value for the last few years, are glad to leave the false world of school behind them. And there they stand: products of 10 years in our education system, reading magazines, playing bingo and watching football matches. These activities might not be harmful in themselves, but to embrace them to the exclusion of everything else is. Why should the majority of children be denied the right to experience and enjoy the greatest achievements of man? Most children are flung into commercial society without picking up a vestige of culture or even understanding of the world in which they live. There is a complete lack of ritual connected with values other than material.

The Crowther Report gives full and detailed examination to the influence of mass-media on the young teenager. Although it does appear that girls are more a prey to this than boys, the influence exists for both sexes. One of the most significant statements in the Report on this subject is:

> The tremendous power of these methods of communication [mass-media] makes it important not to cut short the educational period. Surely society ought not to withdraw from the young worker the help it gave the schoolboy.

The task facing the teacher in trying to combat the powerful forces of commercialised mass-media seems almost impossible. His aim is an obvious one—to try to guide children to discriminate, to evaluate and to reject much of the trash that is poured out on the printed page, over the air and on the TV screen. This task is made well-nigh impossible if the child is to become a worker at 15 and give up the chance of being exposed to any educative forces. To take a simple example—I have seen students reading the *New Statesman* and *New Society* in the Polytechnic Library. Many such students have come from secondary modern schools and probably from what are called "non-bookish" homes, and had they not studied at the Polytechnic in Further Education they might never have come into contact with more worthwhile periodicals at a time when they are maturing and beginning to work out a sense of values.

There is a tremendous idealistic potential amongst young people, but this is not fostered by the cheap superficiality of the comics and magazines which are produced for one reason alone, and that is to make money for the publishers. Norman Collins of ITA has a very poor conception of public demand. He says:

> If one gave the public exactly what it wanted it would be a perfectly appalling service. . . . The overwhelming mass of the letters we get are illiterate, they are ungrammatical, they are deplorably written, and what is more distressing, they evince an attitude of mind that I do not think can be regarded as very admirable. All they write for are pictures of film stars, television stars, or asking why there are not more jazz programmes, why there cannot be more programmes of a music-hall type. I hold the teachers very largely responsible if that is the attitude of people in their teens and early twenties. If we provided simply that it would be deplorable.*

To hold the teacher responsible is scarcely fair while television continues to give the viewers 80 per cent hotch potch of trash. Mr. Cecil King of The *Daily Mirror* is quite honest about his opinion of the reading habits of the British public:

> The trouble is the critics imagine the great British Public is as educated as themselves and their friends, and that we ought to start where they are and raise the standard from there up. In point of fact, it is only the people who conduct newspapers and similar organisation who have any idea quite how indifferent, quite how stupid, quite how uninterested in education of any kind the great bulk of the British Public are.

* Although this remark was made only a few years ago it is interesting to note how out of date it appears—no mention of pop; and jazz, which has earned its place as a serious art form, is lumped together with music hall.

It is pointless to refute these statements even though one is loth to believe in it, but the sales of the *Daily Mirror* and the ratings for the lowest common denominator type of programme show that there is truth in them. The question for every teacher is how long are we prepared to accept the two nations; how long are we prepared to accept so called "high" and "low" culture. Michael Young has given us a salutary warning in *The Rise of the Meritocracy*. We shall continue to have two nations as far as enjoyment of what is valuable and lasting in the arts is concerned as long as we have a system of education where children are segregated at 11 and the majority become young workers at 15. A developing taste for what is good in a child of 16 can be reinforced, but where no initial flowering is possible there can be no strengthening and the child is most vulnerable to the pressures of all that is bad in mass media.

Notes on recent stages in the evolution of pop music

THE term "pop music" refers specifically to the kind of popular music, primarily aimed at young people, that has been in vogue for the last decade and a half. Pop seems to be inextricably bound up with jazz as its main progenitor but inevitably various kinds of folk music and other influences have contributed to its evolution— in short, it is a multi-ingredient musical mongrel. It finds roots in the Romantic musical era of the Victorian age, typified by the dramatic lyrics and music of the great Italian operas. By the turn of the century simple melodies and sentimental lyrics had been churned out by the hundred. These characterised the musical shows in vogue at the time. (Nowadays the contemporary form of this kind of song is usually called "ballad".) Music publishers, street-piano manufacturers and others exploited the popularity of these shows and were soon operating thriving new businesses. However, pop is most of all bound up with jazz.

Jazz was created by a fusion of the rhythmic folk music of the Negro slaves into the harmonic framework of European music. The first jazz bands visited Britain from the USA after the First World War, although they had existed in the coloured communities of the Southern States for some 20 years. In particular in cosmopolitan New Orleans where there was a great deal of musical ability. Negro bands vying with each other for gimmicks began "hotting-up" and improvising on ceremonial marches and popular tunes by drastically altering tempos, using their own ideas of melodic expression and by introducing syncopation.

Jazz acquired widespread popularity among the coloured communities since it reflected the stress, tragedy and occasional moments of happiness the Negro knew in his own life and saw around him.

The liberal approach of the jazz performer to his music enabled him to express with great intensity feelings that could not, or need not, be put into words. The jazz instrumentalist, in effect, would use his instrument as an extension of his own voice to emphasise the "message" that is played or sung. This "message" and the words of the jazz songs provided a sense of unity and strength in the face of the insecurity and unrest engendered by the social deprivation of the Negro communities. Moreover, the powerful cathartic property of the music meant that jazz became a virtually compulsive part of the lives of most who heard it. (It is interesting to note that a similar situation exists today where pop culture provides the teenager, now recognised as one of a distinctive group, with identification and a means of communication and expression.)

In the 1920's white businessmen exploited the appeal of jazz through records. Aimed primarily at the coloured communities, jazz became popular with all Americans. Live performances in clubs, hotels, restaurants, tours and concerts and on commercial radio programmes (which also broadcast records) helped to do this.

The fresh musical vitality of jazz was fused into the idiom of the sentimental pre-jazz era Romantic ballad—itself imported from Europe to become popular in the USA early in the century. From this cross-fertilisation, in the late twenties, sprang an enriched idiom of popular music conceived by a new generation of American ballad writers, among them Cole Porter and George Gershwin. Big dance bands became widely popular during the thirties and forties. Their music had the superficial trappings of jazz which the European ear had grown to enjoy. The commercialised jazz sound was inevitably reflected throughout the whole field of popular music since the ballad singer's musical backing was usually provided by a big band. In this period use of new techniques, particularly musical shows and films, added to those already known since the twenties, led to the commercial expansion of American popular music. New rhythms and dances from Caribbean and Latin American music were also introduced.

The popularity of the big-band idiom continued with a move towards greater orchestral sophistication until the present pop era in the fifties. In Britain in the early forties the revitalised American music gradually supplanted the old-style sentimental ballad. In the late forties there was a revival amongst jazz lovers of traditional jazz ("trad"), i.e. music played by the bands of the twenties.

In 1954 some trad bands included in their repertoires skiffle—a new kind of music watered down from American country-western folk song, country blues and traditional jazz. In a year it became a nation-wide craze amongst teenagers involving them directly with music for the first time. Its appeal was in its do-it-yourself nature; the instruments, washboard, bucket, tea-chest, bass, guitar, etc., could be mostly home-made. At much the same time in America the pop era began with a craze for rock 'n' roll—a renovated form of rhythm and blues, itself a distinctive style of big-band jazz. The character of rhythm and blues—loud, driving and aggressive—was emphasised by heavily accented off-beat drumming, electronically amplified guitars and basses, honking saxophones and powerful blues-shouters; it found a home in the spirit of the post-war years. Rhythm and blues popularised the electric guitar by demonstrating the great musical tension which could be achieved with this instrument. In the early fifties small rhythm and blues groups, making the fullest use of electronic amplification, retained the powerful drive of the big bands and promoted a new kind of dance called rock 'n' roll. The energetic, uninhibited nature of the dance and the music made an overwhelming appeal to the emotionally tense teenager, and the craze spread amongst young people with a vehemence that at times caused minor riots. Rock 'n' roll crossed the Atlantic in the mid-fifties and had the same reception as in America, completely eclipsing skiffle in the process.

Taking note of the explosive appeal of the new kind of music, the entrepreneur concentrated on the teenager who for the first time had money to spend on luxuries. Hence began the present pop era— a whole sub-culture forged on the basis of the "music industry's" exploitation of the teenager. Like skiffle, rock 'n' roll gave the amateur direct participation in music, especially through guitar playing; it had immense emotional appeal for the teenager who idolised the pop stars from the first; it provided him with a sense of strength, unity and security in the face of a seemingly insensitive and hostile adult world. Primarily, it offered a means to communicate across the barriers of personal isolation and a release for pent-up emotions.

The music industry has carefully nurtured the half-predictable emotional appetite of the teenager with the help of ancillary industries (clothes, magazines and comics in particular) along lines indicated in the text of this book and elsewhere. As a result, the pop era has provided a vast commercial success for the entrepreneurs of these industries rather than a true culture of popular music.

The musical idiom of the pop era has been in a state of flux since the advent of rock 'n' roll, as new crazes have come and gone every few years or so. Though rhythm and blues in the form of rock 'n' roll eclipsed it for a couple of years in the mid-fifties, the ballad came back with a fresh appeal aimed at the romanticism of the young person.

Since then, rhythm and blues, the ballad and other styles have competed in a succession of crazes. The early sixties saw a brief craze for trad but in 1962 this gave way to a more sophisticated kind of rock 'n' roll called the twist (old rock 'n' roll plugged as a new kind of dance.) After a year or two the twist, in turn, was superseded by the recent phase of rhythm and blues groups whose music was at first based on American country-blues; in the last year or two the emphasis in pop music has shifted more towards folk music conceived in the shell of the recent style of rhythm and blues.

The shift of emphasis is interesting in that it has been accompanied by the first organic development in pop music since the birth of the era in the mid-fifties. The Beatles have been at the forefront of this pop development and broke away from the stereotyped musical formulae that had characterised pop, with little change, from its birth. The Beatles achieved this by drawing widely on the folk music of several countries and by adopting a more adventurous approach to the harmonic structure of their music (as had the classical ballad writers in the evolution of American popular music during the thirties). In the last year or two The Beatles, and the many pop groups they have influenced, appear to have broken the see-saw popularity cycle of rhythm and blues and the ballad by fusing together elements of the two. Nowadays the distinction between rhythm and blues, folk music and the ballad, is often blurred but the ballad seems to be central to pop music as it was to the music of the pre-pop era. This is probably because in western Europe the essentially melodic character of the ballad is most closely linked with the musical heritage of our society.

In this outline only the two most central influences on popular music, romantic music and jazz, have been considered. Needless to say, many other sources have contributed to the evolution of pop music. These two basic influences continue to cross-fertilise one another, and contributions have come from varieties of folk-music, among them Irish reels, English country dances, minstrel bands (essentially white American imitation of Negro folk music in the nineteenth century) and other folk music from all over Europe.

Latterly, South American and Indian folk music have made their contributions. Again the popular music in Britain and the USA has been considered as this has proved to be of international appeal; however, music popular on a national scale in various European countries has frequently become popular in Britain and the USA.

Questionnaire

Copies of this were sent out to schoolchildren—1223 filled in and analysed.

AGE: ....Years...................Months   Form...................

   1. Do you read any of the following magazines:

      Valentine   Yes/No   Do you read it Regularly/Sometimes
      Jackie   Yes/No   Do you read it Regularly/Sometimes
      Boyfriend Yes/No   Do you read it Regularly/Sometimes

   2. Please give the name or names of any other magazines or comics which you read. ....

....

   3. About how old were you when you started reading any of the magazines or comics mentioned above? ....

   4. If you used to read them and have now stopped, how old were you when you stopped? ....

   5. Do you prefer strip picture stories to printed stories? ....

....

   6. Would you like to have—

      (*a*) More pictures of Pop Stars   Yes/No
      (*b*) More articles about Pop Stars   Yes/No
      (*c*) More strip picture stories   Yes/No
      (*d*) More printed stories   Yes/No
      (*e*) More letters to the Editor   Yes/No
      (*f*) Any other suggestions for improvement?

....

....

7. Is there anything you would like to see taken out?

....

8. Do you buy Pop records yourself? Yes/No. If you answered "Yes", about how often do you buy them? ....

....

9. Do you listen to Pop Stars on the radio? Yes/No. If you answered "Yes", what is the best programme for this? ....

....

10. Do you watch your favourite Pop Stars on T.V.? Yes/No. If you answered "Yes", what is the best programme for this? ....

....

11. If you are reading a book at the moment, would you please give its name, and the name of the author if you know it. ....

....

12. Do you read newspapers? Yes/No. If "Yes" which one? ....

....

Do you read any other magazines or books? ....

....

....

....

....

Comics and magazines mentioned in the questionnaire

Andy Capp
Beano
Beezer
Bimbo
Buster
Dandy
Flash
Hornet
Hotspur
Huckleberry Hound & Yogi-Bear
Hurricane & Tiger
Lion
Rover & Wizard
Smash
Sparky
Topper
TV Comic
TV (Century) 21
Valiant
Victor
War comics:
   Commando, Soldier, Armada, Ace, Fleetway Picture Library
Wham

Bunty
Diana
Judy
June & Schoolfriend
Lady Penelope
Princess

Batman: Batboy
Classics comics

DC comics
Greenlantern
Marvel comics
Monster magazines
Sister Maggie
Superman
Thor
True Crime
Wonder Woman

Boyfriend (now *Trend*)
Jackie
Mirabelle
Petticoat
Romeo
Valentine

Chelsea Newsletter
Mad
Private Eye
Esquire
Life
Reader's Digest
Time

Heartbeat
Love Stories
Red Letter
True Confessions
True Love
True Romances
True Stories

Brides
Flair
Honey
Vanity Fair
Everywoman
Modern Woman
My Weekly
People's Friend
Woman
Woman & Home
Woman's Journal
Woman's Mirror
Woman's Realm
Woman's Weekly

Family Circle
My Weekly
Reveille
Tit Bits
Today
Weekend

Caper
King
Man's World
Man-t-man
Men Only
Mermaid
Modern Man
Parade
Penthouse
Playboy
Skirt
Stag
Swank
Topless
Weekly Strip

Harper's Bazaar
Nova
Queen
She
Tatler
Vogue

Beatles' Monthly
Disc
Disc Weekly
Elvis Monthly

Fabulous
Melody Maker
Music Parade
Music Weekly
Musical Echo
Pop (Mirror)
Rave
Record Mail
Record Mirror
Record Weekly
Rolling Stones Monthly
Showtime
The New Musical Express

Boy's World & Eagle
Knowledge
Look and Learn
Ranger
Round the World
Treasure

Dragster
Hot Rod & Drag Racing
Karting

Autoworld
Autocar
Do it Yourself Car Maintenance
Ford Times
Miniature Autoworld
Model Car Science
Model Cars
Motor
Motorcade
Motor Mechanic
Motor Racing
Motor Sport
Motoring Weekly
Old Time Vintage Cars
Practical Motorist
Popular Motorist
Small Cab Motoring

Canoeing
Getting Afloat
Lightcraft
Model Boats
Motor Boat
Yachting

Aquarist
Athletics Monthly
Boxing Weekly
Charles Buchan's Monthly
Cricket Monthly
Cycling
Football Monthly
Hockey Field
Rifleman
Rowing Magazine
Rugby World
Shooting Times
Soccer Star
The Torch (Southall Swimming Club
    Magazine)
World Soccer
World Sport

Motorbike
Motorcycle
Motor Cycling
Motor Cycle Mechanics
Motor Cycle Monthly
Motor Cycle News
Scooter
Scooter Mechanics
Scooter Monthly
Speedway
Track & Traffic

Angling
Angler's Mail
Angling Times
Creel
Fishing
Fishing Gazette
Fishing Times
Fisherman's Weekly
Fisherman's World
Trout and Salmon

Do it Yourself
Electronics Magazine
Hi-Fi Magazine
Home-Maker
Meccano Magazine
Model Engineer
Model Maker

Practical Electronics
Practical Householder
Practical Wireless
Radio Control

Modern Railway Constructor
Modern Railways
Railway Magazine
Railway Modeller

Aeromodeller
Aeronautics
Aeroplane
Air Cadet
Aircraft Recognition
Airfix Magazine
Air Pictorial
American Aviation
BOAC Aircraft Magazine
Commercial Aviation News
Flight
Flight International
Flying Review
Sud Aviation

Amateur Gardening
Amateur Photographer
Chess Magazine
Dance News
Dancing Times
Hobbies Weekly
Homes & Gardens
Ideal Home
Practical Photographer
Ringing World
Stamp Collector's Weekly
Stanley Gibbons Stamp Monthly

Discovery
New Scientist
Science News
Scientific American
Statist

BB Stedfast
The Brownie
The Guide
The Scout

EMI News
Endeavour (ICI Journal)

Animal Life
Cage & Aviary Birds
Cat's World
Dog's World
Family Pets
Fur & Feather
Horse & Hound
Mainly About Animals
Pony
Riding
RSPCA Magazine

Crusade
Grange Park Baptist Newsletter
The Watchtower

Camping
Camping Club Monthly
The Camper
The Youth Hosteller

Arts Review
Elle
History Today
La Actualidad Espanola

National Geographical Magazine
Paris Match

Pitman's Office Training
Stern
Studio
The Masters

Country Life
Economist
Encounter
European Community
Focus
Forum
Liberal News
Listener
New Society
New Statesman
Poetry
Spectator
The Field
Time & Tide
Which

Exchange & Mar
Photoplay
Radio Times
TV Times

Sources of information

A. BRITTON and M. COLLINS, *Romantic Fiction.*
J. A. C. BROWN, *Techniques of Persuasion.*
G. M. CARSTAIRS, *This Island Now.*
T. CLARKE, *My Northcliffe Diary.*
R. C. K. ENSOR, *England 1870–1914.*
HALL and WHANNEL, *The Popular Arts.*
R. HOGGART, *The Uses of Literacy.*
R. HOGGART, *William F. Harvey Memorial Lecture on the Nature and Quality of Mass-Communications with special reference to Television.*
M. HUTCHINSON, *Educating the Intelligent.*
F. NEWTON, *The Jazz Scene.*
N.V.T., *Report of Conference on Popular Culture and Personal Responsibility* (1960).
V. PACKARD, *Hidden Persuaders* and *Status Seekers.*
R. S. PETERS, *Authority, Responsibility and Education.*
G. H. PUMPHREY, *Children's Comics.*
D. REISMAN, *The Lonely Crowd.*
D. THOMPSON, *Discrimination and Popular Culture.*
E. S. TURNER, *Boys will be Boys.*
DR. F. WERTHAM, *Seduction of the Innocent.*
R. WILLIAMS, *Communications, Culture & Society,* and *The Long Revolution.*
M. YOUNG, *The Rise of the Meritocracy.*
The Writers & Artists Year Book.
Willings Press Guide.
Interview with a contributor to *Jackie.*
Interview with Martin Woolley of Paul Cave Theatrical Enterprises Ltd.
Interview with Pamela Vince, co-author of *Television and the Child.*
Interviews with Newsagents in several London and Middlesex areas.
Interview with Vic Griffiths, guitar and harmonica player in pop group.
Interview with B. A. Williams, Pharmaceutical Chemist, Brentford.
Visits to Cranford Secondary Modern School, Mellow Lane Comprehensive School, Twickenham Girls' School, Gunnersbury Boys' Catholic School.
Discussions with boys and girls who read comics and magazines mentioned.
Interview with Michael Walsh, journalist.
Correspondence with Lloyd Churgin, social worker running boys' club in the Bronx, New York.
Interview with Richard Kell, Poet and English teacher in Further Education.
Analysis of 1223 Questionnaires.

Index